Ex Libris

anemone

Sandra Charters.

A colour guide to familiar

TREES

Leaves, Bark and Fruit

A colour guide to familiar
TREES

Leaves, Bark and Fruit

By Jaromír Pokorný

Illustrated by Jiřina Kaplická

OCTOPUS BOOKS

Translated by Olga Kuthanová
Graphic design: Soňa Valoušková

English version first published 1974 by
OCTOPUS BOOKS LIMITED
59 Grosvenor Street, London W 1

Reprinted 1974, 1975, 1977, 1978 (twice)

© 1973 Artia, Prague

ISBN 0 7064 0288 X

Printed in Czechoslovakia

3/10/02/51–08

CONTENTS

TREES AND MAN

Even though the process of civilization has made man independent of nature and raised him to a higher level, yet he is continually aware of the fundamental influence of nature on generations of mankind.

Plants are a necessary condition of civilization, and of all life on Earth. Without plants, which are capable of producing organic material from chemical compounds and radiant energy from sunlight, there could be no life, no animals, not even man, for they provide the basic source of food and nourishment.

The forest provided primitive man with food, fuel and building material, affording him also protection against enemies and the elements. To realize the importance of trees and forests for man, however, there is no need to go so far back into the past. Even our great-grandfathers could say that trees and their wood were man's companions from birth to death — from wooden cradle to wooden coffin. Man used wood to build houses and make furniture, construct household utensils, tools and vehicles, and shape primitive weapons. Until almost the eighteenth century wood was also the only source of heat and energy. Today, metals, ceramics and plastics made by chemical processes have in many instances replaced wood. But wood's importance and consumption throughout the world is not declining, quite the contrary. Every year the wood from our trees and forests gives us millions of tons of paper and millions of books.

The value of forests and trees, however, does not rest only in the timber they yield. Man is beginning to realize with ever-growing awareness the other functions of the forest and its vegetation. Today we know how important trees and forests are in water management and in preventing soil erosion. And the importance of parks and woodlands for man's health and recreation cannot be over-stressed.

Vegetation, and, above all, trees are also important from the aesthetic viewpoint — refreshing both to the eye and spirit. How bleak and depressing a landscape without trees would be; and what a beautifying and softening effect wisely-placed greenery has, as it enhances modern buildings and constructions. That trees and forests are a source of profound aesthetic experience and inspirations is testified to by the works of prominent writers, painters, composers as well as the motifs of popular folk songs.

Today all civilized nations are making a concentrated effort to protect and increase greenery in cities and countryside. If we are to do a good job of protecting and propagating trees, however, we must know more about them, learn their life secrets and their requirements. Equipped with the necessary knowledge about trees and shrubs we will be better able to select species suitable for a given environment, and will be rewarded by their good and healthy growth.

STRUCTURE OF A TREE

Trees and shrubs are perennial plants whose stems become woody and last for many years. Trees usually have a single erect stem or trunk which at a certain height branches out to form a crown, whereas shrubs branch from near to, or at, ground level. Trees and shrubs are also differentiated according to height. Small trees attain a height of about eight metres, those of the second category fifteen to twenty-four metres, and those of the first category more than twenty-five metres. The thickness of a tree is usually given by the diameter of the trunk measured at breast height, i.e. 1.3 metres above ground.

The trunks of conifers generally extend to the very tip of the slender, conical crown with layers of fairly thin branches usually growing out at right angles. This type of trunk and branching is characteristic of the spruce, fir, Douglas fir and most larches; in the broad-leaved trees it is to be found in the alder and the pyramidal forms of such species as the Lombardy poplar *(Populus nigra)*. The trunks of most broad-leaved trees divide at a certain height into a few, thick, upward-or outward-growing branches which divide further to form the crown which may be broadly oval to round. This shape provides the leaves with the greatest amount of light and air, thus assuring the best conditions for the nourishment of the tree. The tree is anchored in the ground by means of roots which also serve to supply it with water and mineral nutriments.

The complex of a tree's branches and twigs is called the crown, and the trunk or bole and crown combined form a characteristic shape or habit which enables the expert to identify them even from a distance. Frequently, however, the habit is influenced by the environment in which the tree grows and is subject to a certain degree of variation. The most important factor is whether the tree grows in the open or under forest competition. Conifers grown in the open, fully exposed to light and wind, have a conical trunk with a centre of gravity below the mid-point and a crown that reaches almost to the ground. Broad-leaved trees grown under the same conditions have a short, thick trunk with a broad, low-placed crown. Only certain light-demanding trees such as the pine, larch, birch and aspen, have the lower half of the bole clear of branches and the crown placed high even when grown in the open. Trees grown under forest competition are taller with a long trunk and a high-placed crown taking up only one-fourth to one-third of the tree's height. This is mainly the result of shade and associated microclimate. Trees growing on the forest margins have irregular crowns, fully developed only to one side.

The twigs of all trees are covered with buds which, especially in the case of broad-leaved trees which are without leaves in winter, are an important means of identification. Buds are actually embryonic shoots, containing immature leaves or flowers protected by scales. They are differentiated according to their position on the twig. Those appearing at the apex are called terminal and those borne in the axils of the leaves are termed lateral. Lateral buds are either alternate or arranged in a spiral (oak, alder, hornbeam) or in opposite pairs (maple and ash). The positioning of the buds is identical with that of the leaves, in the axils of which they are borne. In other words, a tree with buds arranged in spirals has the leaves also arranged in spirals. Buds are protected against drying out and frost damage by modified leaves known as scales; either by just a single scale (willow or plane tree), two scales (alder), or several scales (beech, hornbeam and oak). Distinguishing features of the scales are colour and pubescence. Some trees that bloom in early spring can be identified by the flower buds, which are of different shapes, e.g. willow, elm, poplar and cherry.

A further good means of identification in some trees are the short, peg-like projections known as spurs (cherry, apple) on which the flower buds are borne. Some trees' twigs have distinctive large or small leaf scars which remain after the leaves fall. The horseshoe-shaped ones of horse chestnut are noteworthy.

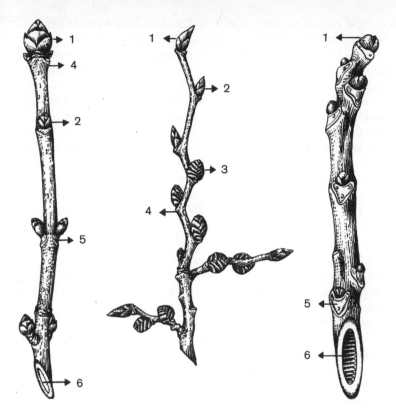

Fig. 1. Twigs of the sycamore, elm and walnut with buds: 1) terminal bud, 2) lateral buds, 3) flower buds, 4) peg-like projections. 5) leaf scar, 6) pith.

Spines and thorns are another good means of identification, e.g. on the twigs of the wild pear, black locust and honey locust. The twigs of other trees have conspicuous lenticels (bird-cherry, white ash), waxy warts (birches) or corky plates (hedge maple and smooth-leaved elm).

Under normal conditions trees are the strongest and fittest members of the plant realm. In comparison with non-woody plants they have the great advantage of height and longevity. Before man introduced intensive land cultivation most of the Earth's surface was covered with forests. Even today the forest would soon reclaim the land, should man cease to tend and cultivate it. This is borne out not only by examples in tropical Africa and southeast Asia, but also by all the lands in Europe that have been left lying fallow. Only where insufficient rainfall, high temperatures or severe winters and frozen soil prevent the growth of trees do they leave such areas to grass, shrubs and succulents.

Nourishment of the Tree

The tree obtains nourishment from the soil through the roots, and from the air through the leaves. Both roots and leaves are adapted by nature for the role they play. The leaves of broadleaved trees consist of the stalk, or petiole, and a thin lamina or blade, which provides the greatest possible surface of contact with the air. Atmospheric carbon dioxide is the tree's main source of food. Together with water and by the means of chlorophyll and radiant energy from the sun it is processed by the leaf cells into organic compounds that go into building the major part of the tree's organs. This process is known as photosynthesis.

Because the amount of carbon dioxide in the air is very low (0.03 per cent on average), the tree has to process great quantities of air. This must take place on the greatest possible leaf surface, which is why the leaves of woody plants are so thin, and why a mature tree has tens or hundreds of thousands of them. To make the most of the sun's energy the leaves are spread out as advantageously as possible, this being aided both by the complex network of branches and by the varying lengths and positions of the stalks.

Another essential element for the life of the tree is water and the dissolved minerals it contains. The tree absorbs the water from the soil through its roots, chiefly through the young parts. From the roots the water passes to minute tubes or vessels, through which it is transported to the trunk. In the trunk these tubes form a continuous column that carries the water to the branches at the very top of the tree. From there it travels via the petioles to the leaf blades where it is distributed by the veins to all parts of the leaf surface. The main force which serves to transport the water to heights of thirty to fifty metres is the cohesion of the water column and the force of transpiration (evaporation). The individual cells and tissues along the way take the amount of water they need for the various chemical processes and the remainder is pulled up to the leaves, where part of the water is used during photosynthesis to manufacture sugar. But a great quantity still remains unused. Woody plants absorb more water than they can use to obtain the necessary amount of mineral substances contained in it; the excess is eliminated by the process known as transpiration. This takes place in the leaves and consists of the evaporation of water, regulated to a certain degree by a system of pores that can be opened or closed. It may also be limited by the curling or drooping of the leaves, and increased by the movement caused by wind. The evaporation of water during transpiration also serves to cool the leaf surface and prevents the leaf tissues from being damaged by high temperatures.

The amount of water transpired by trees into the atmosphere is very great and varies not only according to the size and species of the plants but also according to the conditions of the environment — soil moisture, relative humidity of the air, temperature, strength of the wind, etc. The rate of transpiration of broad-leaved trees is several times greater than that of conifers. The poplar, aspen, alder, birch and ash have a particularly high rate.

Leaves

The leaves of woody plants consist of the stalk or petiole and the lamina or blade. The petiole facilitates movement and positioning of the leaf. The blade is the part where photosynthesis, respiration and transpiration take place. Though all

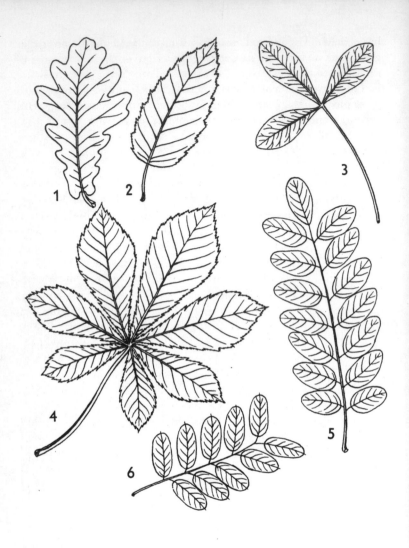

Fig. 2a Types of leaves: Simple leaves: 1) oak, 2) hornbeam.
Compound leaves: 3) golden rain (trifoliate), 4) horse chestnut
(palmately compound), 5) black locust (odd pinnate), 6) pea-tree
(even pinnate).

have the same function, the leaves of the various species differ greatly in shape and size and serve as an important means of identification.

The leaves of broad-leaved trees may be either simple, with a single blade (even if deeply lobed), or compound, with several small blades or leaflets from the same stalk.

Fig. 2b Bipinnately compound leaf: honey locust.

Simple leaves may differ in outline and may be

linear — a narrow leaf with parallel sides, at least 12 times as
  long as it is wide.
acicular — a narrow cylindrical leaf with a pointed tip, needle-like
  in form.
lanceolate — basically, a leaf shaped like the head of a lance, with
  the broadest part below the middle and tapered to a point,
  but never less than 3 times as long as it is wide.
ovate — similar to lanceolate, but always wider, and never more
  than twice as long as it is wide; egg-shaped.
obovate — the reverse of ovate, the stalk rising from the narrow
  end.
orbicular — a rounded leaf as long as it is wide.
cordate — heart-shaped, referring to the lobed base of leaves.
rhomboid — diamond-shaped, or roughly so.

Compound leaves are described as trifoliate if they consist of
three leaflets radiating from a single point. If there are five
or more of these leaflets and if they radiate from the end of the
petiole, the leaf is termed palmately compound. When the
leaflets are arranged laterally in pairs on the main leaf stalk,
the leaf is termed pinnately compound. There may be an odd
number of leaflets with one located at the tip (terminal leaflet),
e.g. the mountain ash, common ash, false acacia (black locust);
or an even number of leaflet pairs, e.g. the honey locust and the
like. In some species with large leaves the leaflets are divided
even further and these are called bipinnately compound leaves,
e.g. the honey locust or Kentucky coffee-tree.

The leaf base may be cuneate (triangular) (durmast oak),
rounded (common pear), cordate (heart-shaped) (lime tree) or
auriculate (eared) (English oak) and the apex acute (birch),
acuminate (slender-pointed) (black poplar), rounded (aspen)
or truncate (blunt-ended) (black alder). The leaf margin may
be either entire (false acacia, magnolia), serrate (cherry, bird
cherry), doubly serrate (hornbeam, grey alder), dentate (crack
willow), or lobed (oaks).

A further distinguishing feature of the leaf blade is the pattern

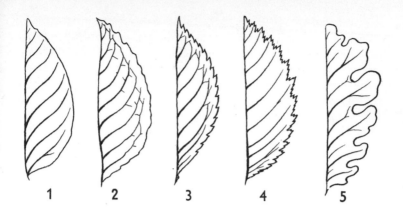

Fig. 3. Leaf margins: 1) entire, 2) sinuate, 3) serrate, 4) double serrate. 5) lobed.

of veins, the system of vascular bundles that supplies the leaf with water and food material. In most woody plants the leaf venation is netted, with a single primary vein and several secondary veins branching off at intervals. The primary vein divides the blade into two, generally equal, halves. In some woody plants, however, the halves are not identical, especially at the base, and these are termed asymmetric (elm, hackberry). In other species the leaf may have several veins branching out from the base (maples); such leaves are usually palmately lobed.

Most European broad-leaved trees are deciduous, in other words, they shed their leaves in the autumn. Only in southern, and in temperate parts of western Europe do some trees retain their leaves throughout the winter, e.g. the common holly, the laurel and the box. In the autumn the organic substances produced by the leaves are concentrated in the body of the tree and the leaves begin to change colour as a result of the decomposition of the chlorophyll and growing predominance of the red and yellow carotenoid pigments, along with the increase of anthocyanin in the cellular sap. This autumnal coloration is characteristic of many species of trees, e.g. the leaves of poplar, birch and common ash turn yellow, the beech turns orange-brown, the red oak and wild service tree turn dull red and the staghorn sumach red or yellow-red. A corky layer forms between the leaf stalk and the twig, severing the connecting tissues. The leaf then falls to the ground, giving back to the soil a substantial part of the minerals taken from it. The shedding of leaves is the result of the climate in these latitudes, where in winter trees other than evergreens limit their life processes to the minimum, eliminating the water in their tissues in order to withstand better the harsh weather of the cold months.

The shape and the structure of the leaves of conifers, called needles, are different. They are narrow, elongate and either rhomboid, semi-circular or elliptical in cross-section in order to limit transpiration as much as possible. This is an adaptation to the environment in which they grow, for they are trees of the north and of the mountains where the climate is harsh and the summer short. To make the best use of this brief period, and not to lose time producing new leaves, they generally retain their foliage throughout the winter. To be able to bear the weight of the snow and survive frost and lack of water, the leaves have a different shape and structure. Most of their cells are thick-walled and their surface is often protected by a waxy layer. They are able to close their respiration pores (stomata) so perfectly that in winter the conifer passes off less water than a leafless broad-leaved tree. However, even conifers do not retain the same leaves throughout their entire lifetime. Depending on the species, leaves may live from 2 to 10 years, the oldest being shed annually. The pine leaves live for a shorter time than those of the spruce; and leaves of a spruce growing at low elevations live longer than those growing in harsh conditions. The process is slow and gradual, and the tree appears unchanged. Only the amount of needles on the ground beneath it serves as an indication of its shedding rate.

Structure of the Trunk

Let us now take a look at the structure of the tree trunk. In the centre, there is a narrow column of pith and around it a continuous shaft of wood, called the xylem. This is made up of concentric circles known as the annual rings. Then comes the thin layer of phloem and, on the outside, the bark, which in older trees may be split and furrowed. Between the xylem and the phloem, there is a thin layer, called the cambium, consisting of several layers of thin-walled cells which, during the growth period, rapidly divide to form new wood on the inside and new phloem on the outside. The annual accretion of wood in our trees is clearly evidenced by the annual rings formed by the varying rate of growth of the cambium, which differs according to the season of the year. In spring, during the period of intensive growth when the trees come into leaf, the cambium produces broad, thin-walled cells called spring wood, whereas the cells produced in the summer are narrow and thick-walled and are called summer wood; during the winter there is no growth whatsoever. The strip of compact summer wood is easily distinguished from the strip of the following year's spring wood so that on a stump we can clearly see the yearly growth, in the form of annual rings, and thus easily determine the age of the felled tree. The width of the annual ring is proportional to the quantity of manufactured food substances, and corresponds roughly to the amount of rainfall and warmth in a given year, i.e. in a favourable year it will be broad, whereas in an unfavourable year it will be narrow. A narrow ring is, therefore, an indication of the unfavourable influence of dry weather and in trees sensitive to the cold of severe frosts, etc. This correlation today forms the basis of a new study known as dendrochronology. By examining the rings in trees hundreds and thousands of years old scientists can determine long-lasting changes in the weather and pinpoint alternating periods of dry and wet years in times about which we have no meteorological data. In trees growing in tropical regions where growth is continuous throughout the year the annual rings are not usually so clearly discernible.

In older trees the outer portion only of the wood is active. The central, internal section of the trunk consists of dead cells and is known as heartwood. The outer live part is called sapwood and this serves as the tree's pipeline for conducting water and other important substances up to the crown. In broad-leaved trees this function is performed by the broad tubular cells, called tracheae, visible in the cross-section as small pores. In conifers these tubular cells are narrower and shorter and are called tracheids.

In the cells and cell walls of heartwood various organic and inorganic substances are stored, e.g. tannins, resins, silicon dioxide, etc. In some trees such as the yew, larch, pine and oak the heartwood is further distinguished from the sapwood by a darker coloration. Heartwood is generally much more durable and of higher quality than sapwood and, in the case of some tropical trees in which the wood is subject to rapid decay and damage by pests, the soft sapwood is hacked off on the spot and only the heartwood is shipped for further processing.

The xylem is surrounded by a thin layer of phloem which conducts the organic substances manufactured by the leaves down to the trunk and roots. It consists of long tubular cells with perforated partitions placed end to end. The surface of the tree trunk is covered with bark which protects it from excessive evaporation, sudden changes in temperature and mechanical damage. Protection against undue evaporation is very important, for great quantities of water are conducted through the outer woody layers.

On the bark we can often see small round or slit-like patches that are slightly raised, and different in colour, from the surrounding bark. These are called lenticels and serve as a path for the exchange of gases between the atmosphere and the living cells inside the trunk and branches.

The bark thickens every year by the addition of a very thin layer of corky tissue. The thickness differs in various trees. Trees growing in the shade usually have thin bark, whereas those exposed to the sun often have thick bark which serves as protection against heat. Old, surface bark layers cannot adapt

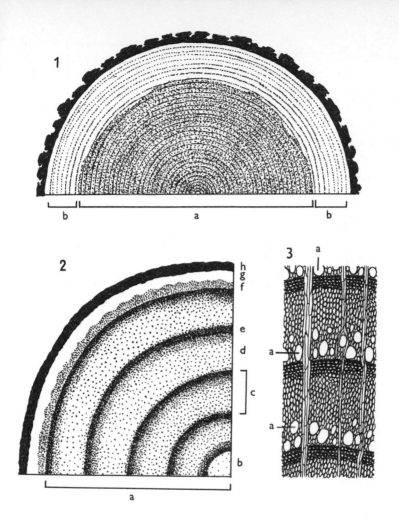

Fig. 4. Structure of trunk: 1) cross section: a - heartwood, b - sapwood, 2) section of cross section: a - xylem, b - pith, c - annual ring, d - spring wood, e - summer wood, f - cambium, g - phloem, h - bark, 3) microscopical section: vessels of the oak.

to the continuous thickening of the trunk and split — usually in furrows or scales. In some trees the bark remains permanently on the trunk (oak, elm), in others it peels off in scales (plane, sycamore), in lengthwise strips (cypress, eastern arbor-vitae) or crosswise strips (birch, cherry).

The Root and Root System

Like the crown, the root system of various tree species has, more or less, a specific, characteristic shape. This is greatly influenced by the environment, and, in particular, the soil. There is also a certain correlation between the size of the crown and that of the root system. For instance, in the case of the spruce, with its thick, conical crown, down which most rain water runs to the ground, the spreading roots branch mostly in the circle circumscribed by the base of the crown, where the soil has the greatest surface moisture. In the beech and oak, where rain falls between the leaves or is conducted along the branches to their tips, the root system is spread out mainly around the trunk. In species which have a high consumption of water the surface roots extend beyond the dimensions of the circle drawn by the crown — as much as fifteen to twenty-five metres from the trunk of a mature aspen, poplar, ash, etc. The depth to which roots grow also varies markedly according to the species. There are trees with deep roots, which, at least in their youth, have what is known as a taproot penetrating to great depths and only a few branch roots, e.g. the Scots pine, juniper, larch, oak, walnut, ash and the like. Another group includes trees that have shallow roots spreading out in a circle and branching in the upper layers of soil, e.g. the spruce, jack pine, frequently the Douglas fir, birch, beech, hornbeam and others. These trees are not firmly anchored in the soil and are easily uprooted by a strong wind. Then there is a third group with a heart-shaped

Fig. 5. Root system: 1) root cap and root hairs, 2) mycorrhiza, 3) root nodules of the alder, 4) taproot system, 5) heart-shaped (cordate) system, 6) widespreading lateral system.

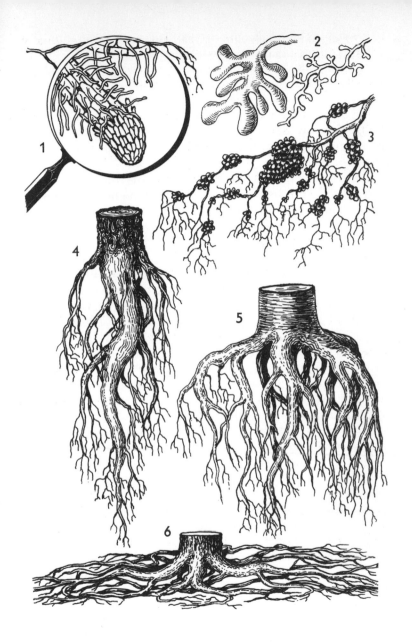

root system. Their roots grow downward at an angle; examples are the fir, lime tree, maple, etc.

As has already been said, the root system is greatly influenced and modified by the environment. In shallow soils over rock, heavy clay soils, or on sites with a high level of underground water, even species whose roots normally penetrate to great depths may have shallow anchorage. Conversely, in humus-rich sandy soils the roots of woody plants which normally spread out may penetrate to greater depths.

Roots anchor the tree in the ground, absorb water and the mineral elements dissolved in it, and serve as storage for reserve food supplies. The structure of the roots is very similar to that of the trunk, only somewhat simpler. Water from the soil is absorbed through the root hairs, which are filamentous out-growths near the tip of each rootlet. The movement of water in the trunk is governed both by the osmotic function of the roots and by the rate of transpiration in the leaves.

Roots aerate the soil and promote the disintegration of the rock substrata. In this they are aided by the carbon dioxide they eliminate as well as by certain chemical substances which break up mineral particles. The nutriments in the soil are also made available by various bacteria and fungi growing in association with the roots. Nitrogen-fixing bacteria that in-crease the nitrogen content of the soil live in nodules attached to the roots of the alder, black locust, honey locust and other woody plants of the pea family (Leguminosae). Most woody plants live in an association, or symbiosis, with fungi whose filamentous growths (hyphae) either encircle the rootlets of the plant (ectomycorrhiza) or penetrate the cells of the root surface (endomycorrhiza). The fungus makes the nutriments in the soil more easily accessible to the tree, besides supplying it with other complex compounds. It receives from the tree substances in return, mainly sugars. Chief ectomycorrhizal associates in the case of forest trees are mushrooms or other mushroom-like fungi. It is well known that certain species of mushroom grow in association with certain species of trees, e.g. the species *Leccinum* is generally found in the company of the birch, aspen and hornbeam, *Boletus* beside the pine, oak, beech and spruce,

Suillus is a companion of the larch, etc. The symbiosis of mush-rooms and woody plants occurs primarily in soils rich in organic substances and raw humus; in soils with insufficient organic matter such a symbiotic association may change to a parasitic one.

Flowering and Reproduction

Like all the flowering plants, trees reproduce and spread naturally by seeds. Some species and garden varieties also produce suckers or shoots directly from the roots, e.g. aspen and some of the elms. Seeds are the sexual means of propagation, formed by the fusion of pollen grains (male cells) and ovules (egg or female cells). Sexual organs in woody plants are contained in the flowers, i.e. organs composed of modified leaves whose function is the production of seed. A complete flower has four different kinds of modified leaves, namely the sepals or calyx, petals or corolla, stamens and pistils. The male sexual organ is the stamen, and is comprised of an anther and filament. When the anther is ripe it bursts and releases the pollen grains, i.e. the actual male cells which are of microscopic dimensions. The pistil is formed of an ovary, containing the ovules, and a stigma, with either a sticky or a hairy surface, to trap the pollen grains. Quite often, the stigma is attached to the ovary by a stalk or style which may be very short, or long and slender. Each pollen grain germinates on the stigma, sending down a tube into the ovary. This tube carries the contents of the pollen grain (nucleus) to an ovule, with which it fuses. After the male and female cells have fused, a seed begins to develop and the ovary eventually becomes the fruit. In conifers the carpels do not fuse to form a pistil and the egg-cells are not enclosed in an ovary but are carried on an ovuliferous scale; trees of this type are called *gymnosperms*.

Flowers containing both stamens and pistils are termed bisexual. Such flowers are to be found in the lime, cherry, false acacia, etc. Flowers containing only pistils, or only stamens, are termed unisexual. These are to be found in all conifers and in most broad-leaved trees that are wind-pollinated (birch, alder,

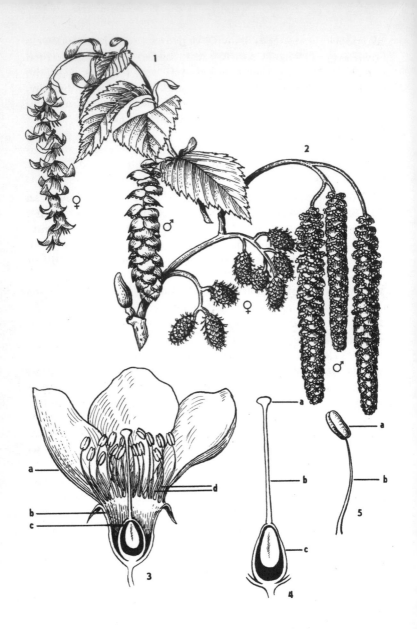

oak, poplar, etc.). Species with both male and female flowers growing on the same tree (spruce, birch, alder) are termed monoecious. Those where either only the male or only the female flowers occur on a single tree (yew, juniper, willow, poplar) are termed dioecious. If both bisexual and unisexual flowers occur, the tree is termed polygamous (ash).

Tree flowers are rarely borne singly. As a rule they grow in clusters (inflorescences), which can contain many flowers or just a few. The commonest types are as follows:

Spike, including Catkin — petalless flowers attached directly to an unbranched stem either erect or pendulous (alder, birch).

Raceme — similar to spike, but each flower having a separate stalk or pedicel (bird cherry).

Panicle — a branched flowering stem bearing several flowers (horse-chestnut).

Umbel — several stalked flowers arising together and forming a flattened or convex head (cornelian cherry).

Dichasium — a branched inflorescence, the branches of which terminate in a flower and two lateral stems, each one of which may also terminate in a flower and further lateral branches.

Corymb — similar to a raceme, but the lower flowers have longer pedicels (stalks) bringing all the flowers up together to form a flattened or convex head (lime).

In addition to these there are various compound flower arrangements comprising several of the various simple types of inflorescence.

The flowers of most trees are much less conspicuous and less brightly coloured than those of shrubs and herbaceous plants. Furthermore, adapted to pollination by wind-borne pollen, they frequently lack, or possess only rudimentary, petals, whose bright colours otherwise serve to attract insects.

Fig. 6. Flowers of woody plants: 1) unisexual flowers of the hornbeam, 2) unisexual flowers of the alder, 3) cherry blossom: a - corolla, b - calyx, c - pistil, d - stamens, 4) parts of the pistil: a - stigma, b - style, c - ovary, 5) parts of the stamen: a - anther, b - filament.

The mode of pollination largely determines the period of flowering of the various species. Wind-pollinated trees such as the poplar, aspen, alder and hornbeam blossom early in spring, before the crown is in leaf, when the pollen can be distributed much more easily. Insect-pollinated trees such as the lime, black locust or cherry blossom later when the crown comes into leaf.

Wind-pollinated plants produce vast amounts of pollen because most of it falls by the way and does not reach the flower and pistil. When the pine or spruce are in bloom huge clouds of pollen are carried by the wind and a layer of yellow dust covers the surface of nearby puddles and ponds. The pollen grains of most wind-pollinated trees have air sacs which make it possible for them to be carried as much as ten to twenty kilometres. In the case of trees without air sacs (larch, Douglas fir, walnut) the pollen grains can be carried only several tens of metres and the trees produce a large number of barren seeds. Trees pollinated by insects produce a far smaller quantity of pollen, as more of the grains manage to reach their intended destination on the body of the insect.

Most plants are protected against being pollinated by their own pollen, for such in-breeding can result in less rugged individuals that are unable to hold their own in the struggle for survival. One such means of protection is the occurrence of male and female flowers on separate trees, another, the blossoming of male and female flowers on the same tree at different periods.

The quantity of seeds produced depends not only on the number of flowers but also on the weather conditions during the period of flowering and seed maturation. Frosts or rainy weather can prevent pollination or fertilization so that few or no seeds are set. Furthermore, some trees do not bear a good crop of seeds every year, for this requires a large quantity of reserve food supplies which the tree must build up over a period of time. Trees producing large seeds and thus requiring larger food reserves (oak, beech, walnut) may only bear them at two to four year intervals. Again, in harsher climates, e.g. in high mountain regions or in the north, where a longer time is

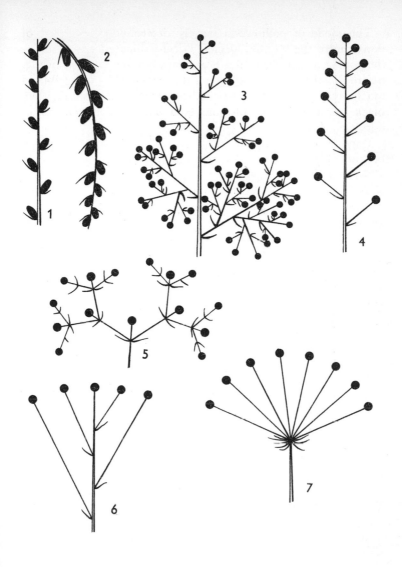

Fig. 7. Types of inflorescence: 1) spike, 2) catkin, 3) panicle, 4) raceme, 5) dichasium, 6) corymb, 7) umbel.

required to accumulate the necessary food stores, the seed-bearing intervals may be longer.

Individual trees start to produce seeds on attaining a certain age, usually one that is fairly advanced. Trees growing in forests usually start some ten to fifteen years later than those growing solitarily. The seed-bearing age of alders, birches and larches growing solitarily is about ten years, that of some maples, the Douglas fir and spruces twenty to thirty, and that of the silver fir and beech thirty to fifty years.

The quantity of seeds in a good year is enormous. One hectare of forest planted with five to fifteen thousand young seedlings will yield up to three million seeds for a pine stand, five million for spruce, three to five million for beech and up to a hundred million for birch. Simultaneously, however, there are great losses both of the seeds and the young plants. Large quantities of seeds are eaten by birds and animals and many fall in places unsuitable for growth where they either do not germinate at all or die shortly after germinating, having used up the store of food in the seed. Similarly, many young trees are destroyed in their first years by drought, frost, invading grass or other plants, or by animals that feed on them. Of the huge crop of seeds, all that usually remains within a few years is less than one per cent per hectare.

To ensure that they fall in a suitable open space and do not merely drop beside the parent tree, where the prospects for their further growth are poor, the seeds are adapted for dissemination to longer or shorter distances. Most are equipped for dispersal by the wind and are either covered with down (willow, poplar) or have membranous wings (birch, elm, pine, spruce) or thick wings (maple, lime, hornbeam). The seeds of another group of woody plants are dispersed by animals, mainly birds. In general these are trees with pulpy, bright coloured fruits which serve as food for the birds, the seeds then being disseminated over a wide area in their excrement (mountain ash, cherry, yew). A third group is formed by seeds which are themselves food for birds and mammals (oak, beech, walnut) and even though most are eaten, some are hidden in a concealed spot as a food store and then forgotten, or else dropped on the way. One would think that seed dispersal by animals is less effective than by wind, but the history of tree migration in the wake of the retreating ice sheet in the period following the Ice Age gives evidence to the contrary. Birch and pine, the first pioneers, were followed by the rapid northward spread of the oak and hazel, whose heavy seeds fall only a few metres from the parent tree. Acorns, however, are a favourite food of jays and pigeons, while hazelnuts are eaten by nutcrackers and woodpeckers and are sometimes carried great distances in their beaks. Naturally, some would drop to the ground while being carried; and thus the offspring of a given tree might take root several hundred metres or even kilometres from the parent. In this way even these trees migrated hundreds of kilometres to the north within a fairly short space of time.

Dispersal of tree seeds by water, as in the case of certain water plants, occurs less frequently. Of the European trees the alder is one whose seeds are dispersed by water as well as by the wind, and of the tropical species the coconut palm is a noteworthy example. The small seed of the alder is equipped with air sacs that keep it afloat on the water surface for weeks until the spring floods carry it far afield. The coconut palm, now found on the shores of continents as well as tropical islands, was brought to these places by sea currents and the regular swell of the ocean. But over long distances man also played a part. Fruits that fall on the shore are carried to the sea by the receding tide, then borne great distances by the currents to be thrown up again by the incoming tide on the shores of other islands and continents.

A closer look at the type of seed, its method of dispersal, and the biological characteristics of a given tree, will reveal that all are closely linked with an efficiency found over and over again in nature. For example, pioneer trees such as the birch, aspen, alder and pine, which are the first to occupy wide, treeless expanses, produce a vast quantity of seeds which are very light and adapted for flights of hundreds of metres or even kilometres. That is how young trees may spring up in places where no other tree is to be found. These trees are also well adapted to the climatic conditions of such localities. They are able to withstand both heat and frost, and have moderate soil requirements, while their rapid early growth enables them to win the battle against surrounding grasses and other vegetation. They begin bearing seeds at an early age and thus rapidly fill the surrounding area with their offspring. On the other hand, shade-tolerant trees such as beech and oak, whose offspring can thrive in shade and appreciate the protection of the surrounding forest in their first years, have heavier seeds that do not fall far.

Fruits and Seeds

The fertilized egg cell develops into an embryo which, with certain reserve tissues, forms the seed which is enclosed in a protective covering called the seed coat. The fruit is a ripened ovary, its walls forming the seed vessel, and contains one or more seeds. In most conifers the seeds are contained in a cone consisting of carpels attached to a central axis that becomes woody.

The fruits of broad-leaved trees are classified as true fruits if their origin is a single ovary, or accessory fruits if other parts of the flower are involved, or if their origin is the entire inflorescence (mulberry). True fruits are further divided into dry and fleshy fruits. Dry fruits with a dry and hard outer wall include the following:

Samara — usually a winged, one-seeded fruit with thin, membranous to leathery coat (birch, elm, ash).
Nut — a one-seeded fruit with hard, woody wall not connected with the seed (hazel, lime, hornbeam).
Legume — usually the product of two carpels splitting along two

Fig. 8. Fruits of woody plants: 1) samara of the tree of heaven, 2) double samara of the maple, 3) nut of the hornbeam and the lime tree, 4) legume of the black locust, 5) capsules of the willow, 6) nut of the butternut, 7) drupe of the cherry tree, 8) pome of the pear tree, 9) berry of the mulberry.

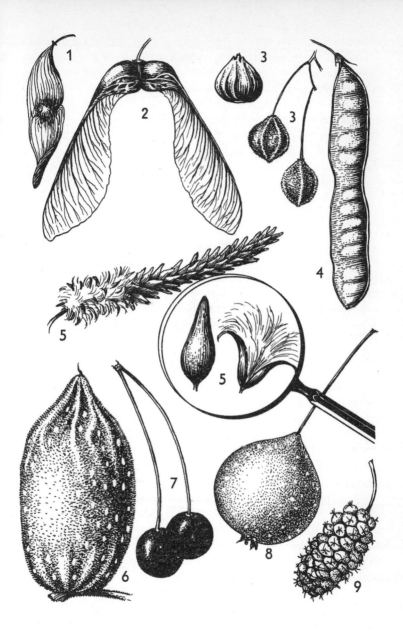

lines of suture when ripe and containing several seeds; characteristic of most members of the family *Leguminosae*.

Capsule — a single or several valved fruit splitting in various ways when ripe and containing several seeds (poplar, willow, chestnut).

Fleshy fruits have soft, fleshy walls. They include:

Drupe — usually a one-seeded fruit with a coat comprising three layers: a thin outer layer, middle fleshy layer and a hard bony layer — the stone encasing the seed (cherry, walnut).

Berry — a fruit with thin membranous covering and fleshy centre with one or several seeds embedded in the pulpy mass; few trees bear true berries.

Of the accessory tree fruits the most common is the pome, a product of the fusion of a fleshy receptacle with ovary wall. The fruit proper is the 'core' containing several seeds. The apple, pear and mountain ash, etc. bear pomes.

The seed is made up of a membranous or hard outer covering — the seed coat or testa — and the inner nucleus, which contains only the embryo and food reserves for the initial period of growth stored in the seed leaves (cotyledons) of the embryo (oak, beech, horse-chestnut, maple, ash, etc.). Some seeds contain a separate food reserve (endosperm) which surrounds the embryo and provides food for its growth (many conifers, etc.). Often clearly discernible on the seed is the scar where it was attached to the fruit. Usually this is light in colour (horse-chestnut and many *Leguminosae*). When germinating, it is through this scar that the seed absorbs the most water and through or near it that the first root and shoot emerge.

Germination takes place if conditions are suitable, i.e. in adequate temperature and humidity. The absorption of water promotes not only the growth of the embryo plant and the rupturing of the seed coat, but also the conversion of the reserve food supplies stored within the seed. The quantity of water the seed absorbs is enormous — 40 to 100 per cent of the dry weight of the seed. Another condition necessary for germination is warmth of a certain degree lasting for a certain period. The minimum temperature required for germination is about 5°C, the optimum about 25°—27°C, depending on the species. Also absolutely necessary for successful germination is an adequate supply of oxygen needed by the seed for conversion of the food stores and for respiration.

If conditions are favourable, the seeds of most woody plants germinate within three to four weeks of sowing. But in some trees the period of germination is longer when sown in spring. If the seeds have become too dry during the winter storage they may not germinate at all, or else not until the following spring. This is true of many seeds, particularly of large seeds or those that fall from the tree in the autumn (silver fir, Douglas fir, white pine, common yew, oak, beech, chestnut, maple, etc.). With these species it is best to sow the seeds in the autumn, or else store them in damp sand at a temperature of 0°—3°C, preferably in a cellar. They are sown together with the sand during the following spring.

Vegetative Reproduction

As already mentioned, there are some trees that multiply asexually, i.e. by vegetative means. In one such example, root suckers, new individuals grow from the roots of the parent tree, which may soon be surrounded by a whole group of young trees. This means of reproduction is found in the aspen, white poplar, black locust, wild cherry, etc. Their root system is usually spread out wide, and the root suckers may appear as far as twenty metres from the trunk. These suckers grow in great abundance, particularly when the parent tree is felled, or when one or more of its surface roots is severed or damaged.

Stump suckers grow from latent or adventitious buds low down on trunks or on root bases, but do not form independent trees unless the original is felled. This ability is not the same in all trees. Conifers generally lack it altogether, and in early youth it is found only in the yew, eastern arbor-vitae and some cypresses. Almost all broad-leaved trees exhibit this ability in youth, but later, after the age of maturity, it disappears in some although it is retained undiminished in others. The group of trees with a constant ability to produce suckers in great abundance includes the willow, poplar, lime, hornbeam, alder, black locust, elm and oak, those with a moderate output include the maple, ash and mountain ash. In advanced age the beech and birch sucker poorly. Suckering of this sort is not important in the wild, since under these conditions, a new individual can spring up only in place of an old tree, from its remains. Man makes far greater use of it in forestry, where over the generations trees are renewed from stumps, and also artificially propagated. In planting new forests, willows and poplars are grown directly from cuttings, as are most ornamental trees and shrubs.

Some trees can also multiply by their pendulous branches touching the soil and sending out roots. Their tips then grow upward, and new individuals are formed. This method is characteristic of the Norway spruce in high mountain areas, the lime growing in stone debris or parks, the arbor-vitae and many ornamental shrubs.

Growth and Age of Trees

The rate of growth of a tree during its lifetime can be charted on a graph. At first, the curve rises until the tree reaches the age when it attains its greatest growth, then it slowly, but continually, falls until it has almost reached the zero level. After this the tree does not grow in height but may thicken in diameter and attain an age of several hundred years. This growth curve is generally the same for all trees, varying only in rate and point of greatest growth, according to the individual species.

Trees are divided roughly into three groups according to their rate of growth — fast, moderate and slow-growing. The first group is distinguished by fast growth in the first years with culmination point at an early age, after which the rate markedly decreases. The tree usually has a short life. Fast-growing trees, therefore, do not attain great heights; on the contrary, these are attained by the moderate and slow-growing species. In slow-growing trees the rate of growth is slower in youth, extends over a greater period of time, and reaches its peak at a more advanced age; the downward curve is more protracted and the tree has a longer life span (fir, spruce, beech).

The tallest and largest trees are the sequoias of North America (*Sequoiadendron giganteum* Buchh. and *Sequoia sempervirens* Endl.), the latter attaining heights of up to 112 metres or more. Heights of 80 to 90 metres are reached by some other west American conifers, e.g. the giant fir, noble fir, Douglas fir and sugar pine. Of the European trees the tallest is the European silver fir with a height of over 62 metres and the Norway spruce, which also attains a height of over 60 metres.

The annual increase in height is fairly rapid in most trees, occurring within the brief period of four to five weeks. Growth begins at the same time as the tree comes into leaf. For the first few days it is slow, then comes a period of rapid growth — one to two centimetres a day — followed by one to two weeks of slower growth, and ending with the appearance of a terminal bud at the tip of the shoot. This way of growth is characteristic of the Scots pine, spruce, fir, ash, beech and many others, the period usually terminating at the end of June. There is, however, another group of trees, whose annual growth is spread out over the whole period of vegetation and lasts from three to four months. Included in this group are the poplar, alder, birch, cypress, larch and dawn redwood. Since the annual growth begins early in spring, usually before the tree's assimilation organs are fully developed, the substances required are taken from the previous year's store; the extent of growth is thus mainly influenced by the weather of the preceding year.

As regards growth in diameter the case is somewhat different. In all woody plants it takes place throughout the period of vegetation, from the time the tree comes into leaf until the leaves fall in the autumn, and the extent is influenced by the weather of the current year. In some trees it equals two to three centimetres in a favourable year. Of the European trees great thickness is attained by the plane, chestnut, oak, lime and sycamore, and of the conifers by the fir and to a somewhat lesser degree by the spruce. The "big trees" *(Sequoiadendron)* of California attain diameters of more than ten metres.

The attainable thickness of the trunk goes naturally hand in hand with the tree's attainable age. There are great differences amongst the individual species. On the one hand, there are the short-lived trees, and on the other, the long-lived ones that live up to ten times longer. The first group includes trees with a more rapid life cycle, which grow fast when they are young, bearing fruit at an early age and ageing soon. This, however, does not mean that they have a short life span compared with that of man. The aspen, goat willow, birch and mountain ash may attain 100—150 years. Twice that age, from 200 to 300 years, is reached by the eastern cottonwood, hornbeam, alder, pine and larch; about 500 years by the beech and sycamore; and 700 years by the spruce and fir. The oldest trees in central and western Europe are the lime, yew and oak, which may live for more than a thousand years. An even greater number of years is attained in the Mediterranean region by the oriental plane, chestnut and the cedar of Lebanon — as many as two thousand; and on the American continent there are trees that are much older. Up to 2500 annual rings were counted on the stump of a redwood and some giant sequoias are 3500 to 3800 years old. About fifteen years ago a stand of bristle-cone pine (*Pinus aristata* Engelm.) was discovered in the Rocky Mountains of Nevada, in which the oldest trees had 4200 annual rings.

The following plates are arranged according to the taxonomic system. The reader, not experienced in systematics, will easily find every described species in the alphabetic index at the end of the book.

Symbols used:
♀ — female flowers
♂ — male flowers

Common or English Yew

Taxus baccata L.

The common yew is a conifer whose distribution has greatly decreased during the past centuries; today it is protected by law in most countries. In the Middle Ages, its wood was widely used to make bows, and, later, costly furniture, and so, with its slow rate of growth, the yew slowly disappeared from the forests. It is now found in broad-leaved woods from England to Greece, eastwards to the western Himalayas and South to North Africa. It is estimated that there are about 30,000 of these trees in Germany. In France it is most abundant in the Vosges and the foothills of the Alps and in Great Britain it can be found from southern England to Scotland and in Ireland.

The common yew can attain a height up to 20 metres, but often it remains only a shrub. It grows very slowly, but may live to the age of a thousand years. It is distinguished by its reddish bark, dark leaves and bright red fruits. The leaves are generally two-ranked, and the inconspicuous flowers, borne on the underside of the twigs, bloom in March. The yew is a dioecious species, and the scarlet, fleshy fruits, which mature in late September and are a favourite food of birds, are borne only on female trees. Today the yew is widely cultivated in parks as an ornamental, including its yellow-variegated and pyramidal form.

Leaves: Flat, 20—30 mm long by 2 mm wide, acuminate, yellow-green on the underside.
Flowers: Female resembling buds, male in yellow, globose heads on the underside of the twig.
Seed: Ovoid, about 6 mm long, enveloped in a scarlet, cup-shaped aril.

1 — ♂ and ♀ flowers,
2 — twig with fruits, 3 — seed and aril, 4 — seed,
5 — bark, 6 — wood

European Silver Fir

Pinaceae

Abies alba MILL.

The silver fir is a tree growing in western, central and southern Europe. In France, it is found at mountain heights (900 to 2000 metres) in the Pyrenees, Alps, Jura and Vosges, and also in the Massif Central. In central Europe, it also grows at lower elevations in hilly country but in southern Europe only in the mountains.

The silver fir is one of the largest of European trees, reaching heights of more than 60 metres in virgin forests and living for five hundred years. Its name is derived from the smooth, silvery-grey bark. The buds are non-resinous. The needles are arranged in two opposite ranks on the twig, leaving a circular leaf scar upon falling. The yellow male flowers are clustered on the underside of the previous year's shoots, the female flowers, resembling small green candles, are borne on the upper part of the crown. By autumn they develop into cylindrical cones that mature in late September and then disintegrate. The European silver fir grows well in shade when young, but requires moist soil and clean air, and is susceptible to severe winter frosts. In drier climates, and in areas with polluted atmosphere, it is on the decline. It is, therefore, not suited for planting in city parks. The wood is soft and light and is used mainly in the building industry.

Needles: Flat, bluntly notched at the tip, 15—30 mm long by 2—3 mm wide, with two whitish bands below.
Cones: Cylindrical, 10—20 cm long by 3—5 cm wide.
Seed: Triangular, 1 cm long with large triangular wing.

1 — ♂ flowers,
2 — ♀ flowers,
3 — twig, 4 — cone, 5 — seed scale, 6 — seed, 7 — bark

Douglas Fir

Pseudotsuga menziesii FRANCO

The Douglas fir is a native of North America growing from California up to British Columbia. It was introduced in Europe in 1828 and is widely cultivated today in the woods and parks of western and central Europe because of its rapid growth and high quality wood. It is a large tree, attaining heights of 50 metres and double this in its homeland. It is easily recognized by the sharp-pointed, reddish-brown buds and ovoid cones, with three-lobed, exserted bracts. The needles are flattened, and stand out all around the twig. The bark of old trees is divided into thick ridges separated by deep fissures. The Douglas fir likes partial shade, and is adapted to a long vegetation period and light frosts. It finds optimal conditions in areas with a coastal climate, in Great Britain, Denmark, northern Germany and France.

The related form *Pseudotsuga glauca* Mayr. grows in the Rocky Mountains at heights above 2000 metres. It has a thinner and less deeply furrowed bark, blue-green needles and cones with reflexed bracts. It has a slower rate of growth and is more suitable as an ornamental.

Needles: Flattened, with two greenish-white bands at the base, 20—35 mm long by 1.5 mm wide; when crushed between the fingers they give off a sharp scent.
Cones: Ovoid, with three-lobed exserted bracts, 5—10 cm long by 2—3 cm wide.

1 — ♂ flower,
2 — ♀ flower,
3 — twig,
4 — underside of twig, 5 — buds,
6 — cone,
7 — seed,
8 — habit

Common or **Norway Spruce**

Picea abies KARST

The Norway spruce is a typical tree of the mountain forests of central Europe and the northern European taiga. It has a narrow, conical crown with branches arranged in regular whorls, and grows to heights of more than 40 metres, in virgin stands up to 60 metres at the age of 400 to 700 years. The bark is brown and furrowed. The leaves, rhomboid in section, are borne on peg-like projections, a typical characteristic of all spruces, which give the twig a rough surface when the leaves have fallen. The female flowers resemble small, erect reddish "candles" at first, but later change into pendant brown, elongate cones. The winged seeds are shed on warm and windy spring days.

The Norway spruce has a fairly shallow and spreading root system and is, therefore, easily uprooted by strong winds. It does not require a warm climate and is resistant to frosts. Its range in Europe extends to the polar regions and to altitudes up to the tree line. In hilly country it prefers cool and shady valleys. It grows well in shade but requires fertile soil and moist air. It is marked by great variation and occurs in a number of different forms. The soft and flexible wood is widely used in the building industry, and the bark yields tannins.

Needles: Quadrangular, pointed, lustrous green, 10—25 mm long by 1 mm wide.
Flowers: Male yellow, clustered in catkins; female flowers red or green cones.
Cones: Cylindrical, 8—16 cm long.
Seed: Coffee-brown.

1 — ♂ flowers,
2 — ♀ flowers,
3 — twig, 4 — cone, 5 — seed,
6 — twig without leaves, 7 — bark,
8 — habit

Common or European Larch

Larix decidua MILL.

Pinaceae

The larch is the only European conifer that is deciduous, shedding its leaves in autumn. It is a native of the Alps, Sudetens and Carpathians, but today is cultivated throughout practically the whole of Europe. It attains heights of 40 metres and has a thin, high-set crown. In old trees the bark is thick and deeply furrowed. The fresh green needles are borne singly on one-year shoots, and in clusters of 25 to 40 on older twigs. The tree flowers in early April, one of the first conifers to do so. In the autumn it is covered with ovoid cones which remain on the tree for several years. The larch begins producing seeds by the time it is fifteen years of age.

The larch is a sun-loving, fast-growing tree that requires abundant light and clean air. It is resistant to frost (except when the leaves are young) and heat, and its large, cordate root system provides it with firm anchorage. It is a very attractive tree, especially with the fresh, green foliage of spring.

The wood is of high quality, with a great expanse of reddish-brown heartwood. It is very durable and is much used in the building of boats, wall-panelling, light furniture, wooden staircases, etc.

Needles: Soft, 15—30 mm long, borne singly on one-year shoots and in clusters on older twigs.
Flowers: Female purplish red (sometimes green), male yellow.
Cones: Ovoid, 1—3 cm long.
Seed: Light brown, 4 mm long.

1 — ♂ and ♀ flowers,
2 — twig with cone, 3 — seed,
4 — habit,
5 — wood

Scots Pine

Pinaceae

Pinus sylvestris L.

The Scots pine is widespread throughout most of Europe from Spain and Greece to the Polar Circle in the north, and to Siberia in the east. It is an important ornamental as well as forest tree. It attains heights of 30 to 40 metres and the crown is placed high up on the trunk. The bark is thick and furrowed on the lower part of the trunk and an attractive orange-brown on the upper part. The deep root system provides it with good anchorage, making it possible for it to grow even on steep, stone cliffs and in sandy situations. The needles grow in pairs. In May the reddish female flowers appear at the tips of the new shoots; the yellow male flowers are borne in clusters on the previous year's shoots. The woody cone does not attain its full size until the autumn of the second year and releases the winged seeds on dry windy days at the end of the winter.

The Scots pine thrives in almost any climate and in poorer and drier soils. That is why it may be found on sandy or shallow soils that other more demanding trees find unsuitable. The wood is light and of good quality, the heartwood pale brown — used for columns, windows, doors, sleepers, etc. In some places its resin is used by the chemical industry.

Needles: Stiff, growing in pairs, 3—7 cm long by 1.5—2 mm wide.
Flowers: Female in small reddish stalked cones, 1 cm long, male yellow, ovoid.
Cone: Ovoid, 3—7 cm long with mat grey apophyses.
Seed: Variously coloured, 4 mm long, with sword-like wing.

1 — ♂ flowers,
2 — ♀ flowers,
3 — twig with maturing cone,
4 — cone,
5 — seed,
6 — bark

50

1 ♂ 2 ♀ 3 4 5 6

Swiss Mountain Pine

Pinaceae

Pinus mugo TURRA

Swiss mountain pine has two different forms — the tree form growing to heights of 10 to 20 metres, and the shrub form, 2 to 4 metres high, called the mountain dwarf pine. The Swiss mountain pine, as its name implies, grows mainly high up in the mountains near the tree line; it is also found in the foothills in peat-bogs. The tree form predominates in the western Alps, Vosges and Pyrenees, the shrub form is more abundant in the eastern Alps and Carpathians.

Its leaves greatly resemble those of the Scots pine but are arranged more densely on the twig. The tree form differs from the Scots pine in having grey-black, furrowed bark, which goes all the way up to the crown, and asymmetric cones with knoblike, red-brown scale tips. In the shrub form the cones are symmetrical, broadly opened, with red-brown scale tips.

The Swiss mountain pine is a sun-loving tree that thrives in poorer, shallower soils. Its chief importance is as protection against avalanches and soil erosion. The decumbent form is very popular as an ornamental tree.

Needles: In pairs, 3—8 cm long, densely clustered on the twig.
Flowers: The same as in Scots pine.
Cones: Spherically ovoid, 2—5 cm long, lustrous brown. In the Swiss mountain pine the cone is asymmetrical with knoblike scale tips.

1 — ♂ flowers,
2 — ♀ flowers,
3 — twigs,
4 — cone of Swiss mountain pine,
5 — cone of mountain dwarf pine, 6 — seed

Arolla Pine

Pinus cembra L.

The Arolla pine is a high mountain tree growing in the Alps and Carpathians near the tree line at elevations of 1500 to 2400 metres, in areas with a brief, hot summer. It grows to a height of about 25 metres or more but its knotty trunk and thick ovoid crown reaching almost to the ground are an impressive sight in the harsh alpine environment, where a forest is hard put to keep a foothold.

The Arolla pine has thick, rust coloured, downy shoots and needles clustered densely on the twigs. The cones take two years to mature and when ripe in September they fall to the ground where they disintegrate. The sweet oily seeds are a favourite of birds and rodents. New individuals grow from the seeds they drop on their way, often far from the parent tree. The Arolla pine has a slow rate of growth; not until after its sixtieth year does it begin to flower and bear fruit, but it attains an age of several hundred years. It is adapted to the harsh, mountain climate and stands up well to frost, windstorms and heavy snow. The wood is strong and light, and was formerly used to make furniture and carved objects. Because of its fairly infrequent occurrence, however, it is now a tree protected by law, and an attractive ornament of our high mountains. The related form *Pinus cembra sibirica* Rupr. grows in Siberia.

Needles: 5—12 cm long, in clusters of five.
Cones: Ovoid, 5—8 cm long and 3.5—5 cm wide, purplish-brown, with terminal umbo.
Seed: About 1 cm long, wingless, slightly angular.

1 — ♂ flowers,
2 — ♀ flowers,
3 — twig,
4 — cone,
5 — seed scale,
6 — seed

Weymouth or Eastern White Pine

Pinaceae

Pinus strobus L.

The Weymouth pine is a native of the United States and Canada and was introduced into Europe by Lord Weymouth in 1705. Today it is widely cultivated throughout the western, central and eastern parts of the Continent. It attains heights of up to 40 metres or more. The bole is straight and is topped by an irregularly shaped, layered crown with soft, silky grey-green foliage that is very attractive. The young tree has smooth green bark that becomes rough and fissured with age. The cones mature in the second year and immediately shed the seeds in September.

The Weymouth pine grows rapidly and well up to the age of a hundred years. It is very resistant to frost, requires moderate light and thrives in moist, light soils. It has proved excellent in the improvement of poor, degraded soils, and does well even in city parks. Its most serious enemy is the disease caused by the fungus *Peridermium strobi*, which produces resinous blisters on the trunk, retards growth and may even kill the tree. The Weymouth pine yields light, brownish heartwood used in making doors, window frames and other products of the carpenter's trade.

Shoots: Thin, bare.
Needles: Slender and soft, 6—14 cm long, in groups of five.
Cones: Elongate, 8—20 cm long with prominent scale tips bearing a rounded projection.
Seed: 5—6 mm long, marbled brown, winged.

1 — ♂ flowers,
2 — ♀ flowers,
3 — one-year cone, 4 — twig,
5 — cone,
6 — seed

Jack Pine

Pinus banksiana LAMB

The jack pine is widespread in Canada and the north-eastern United States, where it grows chiefly on poorer, sandy soils. It was introduced into Europe in 1785. In the late nineteenth century it was widely planted as a forest tree because of its resistance to fungus diseases, and its rapid growth in youth. However, it was found that after the fortieth year the rate of growth declined rapidly and the bole became crooked; so the initial enthusiasm soon waned.

The jack pine reaches a height of only about 20 to 25 metres and has a relatively short life span, about a hundred years. It forms two whorls of branches each year. It differs from the Scots pine in having short, pale-green needles, black bark with scaly ridges extending up to the crown, and small, strongly incurved cones. These remain on the tree for many years and open only if high heat is applied, often not until after a forest fire. This fact, as well as its ability to thrive in poor soils, is why it so rapidly seeds and covers large areas destroyed by fire. In Europe the jack pine can be recommended only as a short-term pioneer tree in extremely poor and degraded soils, in dry areas, to improve and prepare the soil for more demanding trees.

Needles: Pale green, in pairs, 2—5 cm long.
Flowers: Female carmine, male yellow.
Cones: Pale brown, strongly incurved, 3—5 cm long, remaining unopened on the tree for many years, scale tips flattened.
Seed: Black-brown, 3—4 mm long.

1 — ♂ flowers,
2 — ♀ flowers,
3 — twig,
4 — needle,
5 — cones,
6 — seed

Austrian Pine

Pinus nigra ARN.

The Austrian pine is a native of the Mediterranean countries, Spain, Calabria, Corsica, Balkan Peninsula and Asia Minor. The natural northernmost limit of its distribution was originally Austria, but today the Corsican and Austrian varieties especially are widely cultivated for their rapid growth, and high quality wood, in western and central Europe.

The tree attains a height of 40 metres and has a straight bole which, however, tends to be very knotty. It differs from the Scots pine in being more darkly coloured, with black-brown, furrowed bark extending to the dense crown with dark green foliage. The cones mature in the second year. The Austrian pine thrives in areas with mild winters and hot summers, especially in lime-rich soils. It does not require much moisture and is used to afforest karst territories and to strengthen sandy sea dunes in maritime countries. The wood is resinous and especially well suited for boat building. In some places where there are large forests, use is made of its resin.

Needles: Dark green, in fascicles of two, 8—16 cm long.
Cones: Ovoid, 4—8 cm long, with lustrous, yellow-brown, rounded scale tips.
Seeds: Varying in colour, 5—7 mm long, winged.

1 — ♂ flowers,
2 — ♀ flowers,
3 — twig with cone, 4 — needles,
5 — seed,
6 — bark

American Arbor-vitae or **White Cedar**

Thuja occidentalis L.

Cupressaceae

This tree is a native of the eastern United States and Canada, where it is found mainly in river valleys and moderately swampy sites. It was introduced into Europe as early as 1540 and today is widely cultivated there, especially in parks and cemeteries. The growth rate is slow and the tree attains a height of only 20 metres or so, with oblong crown reaching to the ground. The grey-brown furrowed bark peels in narrow, longitudinal strips. The terminal shoot stands erect, the lateral branchlets are more or less horizontal. The leaves are scale-like and grow in twin pairs closely pressed to each other. The upper-surface of the twig is dark green, the under-surface yellow green without markings. The inconspicuous flowers are borne at the tips of the branchlets. The oblong cones, 7 to 10 mm long, open in October to release the small, winged seeds.

The tree is very resistant to frost and tolerates both shade and pruning well. It is used to form all green hedges. In sunny situations it is affected by changes in temperature, and sometimes frost causes it to dry up. Its many ornamental forms make it particularly desirable for park landscaping.

Leaves: Scale-like, growing in pairs, the tips of lateral needles curved inward.
Flowers: Female greenish, 2 mm long; male grey-green.
Cones: 7—12 mm long with 3 to 5 pairs of scales.
Seed: Two-winged.

1 — twig with flowers,
2 — undersurface of twig, 3 — cone,
4 — seed,
5 — shape (habit),
6 — bark

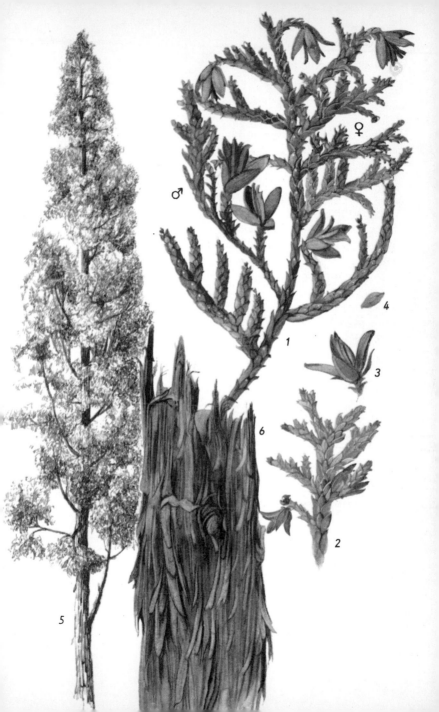

Lawson Cypress

Chamaecyparis lawsoniana PARL.

Cupressaceae

Members of this genus are natives of North America and Asia. Best known in Europe is the Lawson cypress, introduced there from America in 1854. It has a narrow, conical crown and reaches a height of up to 60 metres. It greatly resembles the arbor-vitae but differs from them in having pendulous terminal shoots, with reddish-brown, scaly bark, narrow white markings on the underside of twigs, and scale-like needles. The greenish female flowers are borne on the tips of the shoots. The cones, green at first, mature in September when they open to release the small, winged seeds.

The Lawson cypress is indigenous in California and Oregon, where it grows in mountain valleys alongside streams and brooks up to elevations of 1500 metres. Young trees grow well in shade, older ones require more light. It thrives best in well-drained but moist soils. In Europe, it is cultivated mainly as an ornamental in parks, forestry plantations being mainly experimental and of small area. The wood is light and durable, and particularly well suited for underwater constructions. Of the Asian cypresses, the one most commonly found in Europe is the sawara cypress (*Chamaecyparis pisifera* Sieb et Zucc.), which has a great number of ornamental forms.

Leaves: Scale-like, growing in opposite pairs.
Flowers: Male purplish red, female green.
Cones: Globose, 6—8 mm in diameter, composed of 8 umbrella-shaped scales.
Seed: Flat with broad lateral wings.

1 — ♂ flowers,
2 — ♀ flowers,
3 — twig,
4 — twig (enlarged),
5 — seed,
6 — cone,
7 — shape (habit),
8 — bark

1   2   3   4   5   6   7   8   ♂   ♀

Juniper

Cupressaceae

Juniperus communis L.

The juniper is extremely adaptable to various climates and grows in most of Europe and a large part of Siberia. It grows in poorer, drier soils and thus may be found both on dry limestone slopes as well as in damp, acidic soils, both on lowland and on mountains. It requires ample light for good growth, however, and therefore generally grows in pastures, margins of woods, heaths and non-fertile soils. It occurs mostly as a shrub, less frequently in tree form, growing to a height of 10 metres. Its sharp, prickle-pointed leaves are slightly grooved, and have a whitish band on the upper surface. The juniper is a dioecious species, i.e. individual trees bear only male, or only female flowers. Inconspicuous, they are borne in the axils of the needles, maturing after two years into blue-black berry-like cones. The juniper is highly valued in forestry as a pioneer and to prevent soil erosion. In garden landscaping its dwarf forms are mainly used in rock gardens. The high quality wood is of little importance since the tree is of such small dimensions. The berries are used for flavouring gin and seasoning food.

Leaves: Sharply pointed with white band on the upper surface, 10—15 mm long, in whorls of three.
Flowers: Male yellowish, 4 mm long, female greenish.
Cone: Berry-like, ovoid, 5—8 mm across, blue-black.

1 — ♂ flowers,
2 — ♀ flowers,
3 — berry,
4 — seed,
5 — habit

Aspen

Salicaceae

Populus tremula L.

The aspen is a forest tree, occurring widely through-out the whole of Europe, and extending beyond the Arctic Circle in the north. In central Europe it grows in lowland and on mountains up to and above 1000 metres; it is most plentiful, however, in hill country, coppice forests and forests which are clear-felled.

It reaches heights of 25 to 30 metres and has a sparse, highly placed crown. The bark is smooth and coloured greenish grey, but old trees have fissured blackish bark at the lower part of the trunk. The buds on the twigs are lustrous-brown and sharply pointed. The aspen is a dioecious species (male and female flowers on separate trees). It flowers in March and the tiny seeds, imbedded in cottonwool-like hairs, are shed in late May. The leaf stalk is long and flattened, and even a slight breeze sets the leaf in motion. The aspen is a light-demanding tree and does not require rich soil. The seeds are carried vast distances, thus making this a pioneer tree in clearings, pastures and fallow land. It also propagates well by root suckers. The wood is light, splits easily and is used to make matches, roof shingles and cellulose.

Leaves: Orbicular, 2.5—7 cm long, margin coarsely toothed.
Flowers: Male in brownish-red catkins, female in green catkins.
Fruits: Capsules arranged in spikes.
Seed: Small, covered with white cottony down.

1 — ♂ flowers,
2 — ♀ flowers,
3 — fruits,
4 — leaves,
5 — bark

White Poplar

Populus alba L.

The white poplar grows in moist lowland woods, sometimes by the waterside. It extends from Spain through central Europe to southern Siberia, growing to heights of up to 30 metres. It has a thick trunk topped with a broad rounded crown, and the bark is smooth and greyish, but blackish and fissured at the base. The annual shoots are covered with whitish-grey down, including the small buds. The dioecious flowers appear at the end of March and the seed capsules burst in May. The white poplar propagates also by means of root suckers growing from the lateral roots, often as far as twenty metres from the trunk.

The white poplar grows in regions with a mild climate. It requires abundant light and ample moisture, and stands up well to flood water and slightly acidic soils. It is very attractive as an open-grown tree in water meadows, and, because of its vast root system, is used also to strengthen sand dunes. In intensive forest management it is being replaced by cultivated forms of black poplars. The wood is soft, and used to make cellulose and for turnery. The pyramidal form from Turkestan, known as *Populus alba pyramidalis* (syn. *bolleana*), often makes its appearance in parks.

Twigs: Whitish, tomentose.
Leaves: Palmately five-lobed, (3) 6—10 cm long, white-tomentose on the underside.
Flowers: Similar to those of the aspen.
Capsules: Arranged in spikes, 6—10 cm long.
Seed: 1 mm long.

1 — ♂ flowers,
2 — ♀ flowers,
3 — twig with leaves and fruit,
4 — habit

2 ♀   ♂ 1   3   4

Black and **Lombardy Poplars**   *Salicaceae*

Populus nigra L.

The black poplar's natural range of distribution embraces the whole of western, central and eastern Europe, extending into Siberia as far as the Yenisei River. It grows in moist soils, often alongside large rivers, mainly on sand and gravel formations. It is a large tree, attaining a height of 35 metres, with a widespreading crown. The trunk is covered with thick, furrowed, grey-black bark. The twigs and buds are yellowish. The leaves, broadly wedge-shaped at the base, are arranged alternately on the twig. The catkins flower in April and the capsules shed the downy seed in early June. The black poplar is a tree of riverine forests and requires abundant light and a high level of underground water for good growth. In commercial forests it is today being replaced by the Carolina poplar (*Populus canadensis* Moench.), a hybrid between the black poplar and the northern cottonwood *(P. deltoides)*. It is distinguished by rapid growth and is cultivated in plantations. The black poplar produces abundant, stump suckers and is also propagated by cuttings. The pyramidal form *Populus nigra italica* (syn. *pyramidalis*), the Lombardy poplar, is widely planted in parks and alongside highways. The light wood is used to make plywood and cellulose.

Leaves: Rhombic-ovate, 4—10 cm long, with acuminate apex and coarsely toothed margin. Stalk without glands.
Flowers: Male catkins carmine, female catkins greenish brown.
Fruit: Capsules arranged in spikes, 10—15 cm long.

1 — ♂ flowers,
2 — ♀ flowers,
3 — buds,
4 — leaves and fruits, 5 — habit of the Lombardy poplar

Balsam Poplar

Populus balsamifera L.

The balsam poplars are indigenous to North America and Asia. The one most commonly cultivated in Europe is *Populus balsamifera* L., a native of North America, where it grows on alluvial bottomlands in the northern United States and in Canada. The name is derived from the pleasant balsam smell of the opening buds and leaves. It grows to a height of 30 metres and has yellow-grey bark, thick and furrowed, and coloured blackish at the base of the trunk. The twigs are yellow-brown to brown, the buds covered with a layer of balsam resin. The flowers and fruit are very much like those of the white poplar. The balsam poplar is a light-demanding tree that requires considerable moisture. In Europe it is cultivated mainly in parks for its ornamental, light-coloured bark and pleasant scent in spring. Planted occasionally in hill country is the western balsam poplar (*Populus trichocarpa* Torr. et Grey), a native of western North America. A northern Chinese poplar (*Populus simonii* Carr.), a native of China and Manchuria, is more frequently planted as a street and shade tree in European cities. It is an attractive ornamental, with whitish bark, and nearly rhombic, 6 to 10 cm long leaves, which appear on the tree in early spring.

Leaves: Ovate, with rounded base, whitish green blotches on the undersurface, 5—12 cm long.
Flowers: Male and female catkins 8—12 cm long.
Fruit: Capsules loosely arranged in spikes 12 cm long.

1 — ♂ flowers,
2 — ♀ flowers,
3 — leaves and fruits, 4 — buds

White Willow

Salix alba L.

The white willow is the commonest tree-size willow in Europe, attaining heights of 20 to 25 metres with trunks one metre across and living from 80 to 120 years. Old trees have thick, vertically furrowed, yellow-brown bark. The yellowish flowers, arranged in catkins, appear in April, while those borne on the female trees ripen into capsules with small, down-covered seeds in early June.

The white willow is found mainly in lowland woods alongside rivers where, together with poplars and alders, it grows on sites with a high water table. It stands up well to prolonged spring floods. Its range of distribution embraces most of Europe, eastwards to western Asia and southwards to North Africa, mainly in the valleys of large rivers. It is a light-demanding tree, resistant to frost, and does well even in heavy and acidic soils. It is marked by the vigorous production of stump sprouts. In practice, it is propagated mainly by cuttings which root readily. The wood is soft, light and flexible and is used mainly for the building of boats, making wooden shoes, cellulose and cricket bats; the supple young stems are used for basketwork. Frequently planted in parks and cities is the hybrid between *Salix alba* and *S. babylonica* known as *S. x chrysocoma*. This has slender pendulous branches reaching to the ground and is the commonest of several kinds of "weeping willow".

Leaves: Narrow lanceolate, 5—10 cm long by 1—2 cm wide, with finely toothed margins and silky hairy on the undersurface. *Flowers:* Male yellowish, female greenish, borne in catkins 3—5 cm long. *Fruit:* Capsules with small downy seeds.

1 — ♂ flowers,
2 — ♀ flowers,
3 — buds,
4 — leaves and fruits, 5 — bark

Crack Willow

Salix fragilis L.

Salicaceae

The crack willow is widespread throughout most of Europe, extending northward as far as the middle of Sweden and Norway. Like the white willow it grows mainly beside rivers and brooks in moist situations but, unlike the former, occurs also at higher elevations — up to 600 or 700 metres. It grows more slowly, and attains heights up to 25 metres. The trunk is frequently crooked, the bark of young trees being smooth and grey-green, the buds pressed close to the twigs. The lateral branches break off easily at the junctions, hence its name. The leaves are lustrous-green above, blue-green beneath. The dioecious flowers, borne in catkins, appear in April, and the capsules release the small downy seeds in early June. The crack willow is marked by vigorous propagation by sprouts. Often growing alongside brooks near villages are the so-called pollarded willows, the result of cutting-back the trunk and of repeated cutting of the branches over a period of 2 to 5 years. In practice, new individuals are propagated by cuttings. The crack willow interbreeds easily with the white willow and other willows and therefore one is more likely to come across hybrids than the pure species in the wild. The wood is used for cricket bats, and the young shoots for making baskets.

Leaves: Lanceolate, 6—15 cm long, broadest in the lower half as a rule, with blue-green undersurface and toothed margin.
Catkins: Yellow-green, 2.5—7 cm long.

1 — ♂ flowers,
2 — ♀ flowers,
3 — leaves and fruits, 4 — habit,
5 — bark

Goat Willow or Great Sallow

Salix caprea L.

Salicaceae

The goat willow is more abundant in forests than any other willow. Its range includes all of Europe and extends far into Asia. It grows from lowland to high mountain elevations and, unlike other willows, is an important pioneer in forests where its seedlings colonize forest clearings and felled areas. The goat willow is a shrub or small tree 3 to 10 metres high with a broad, broom-shaped crown. It reaches an age of 40 to 60 years or more. The bark is smooth and grey, with rhomboid lenticels. The twigs are stout, the buds ovoid, and the branches with their large catkins, that appear before the leaves, are popular heralds of spring, being among the first wild flowers to be sold at flower stalls. During the flowering period in March the goat willow is a very attractive ornamental, male individuals resembling a large yellow bouquet at this time. It provides bees with their first feast of the year. The seed ripens and is shed in May. At the base of the leaf stalk are small semiheart-shaped leaf-like bodies (stipules) which soon fall.

This tree is propagated, both in the wild and artificially, by seed, as cuttings root very poorly. It is a frost-resistant species that thrives in poorer and drier soils. The goat willow is an important pioneer tree in forestry, and animals are fond of nibbling its bark.

Leaves: Broadly ovate, 5—10 cm long, with sinuate margin, grey, downy beneath with prominent veining.
Flowers: Dioecious; male catkins yellow, 2—3.5 cm long, erect, female grey green, 3—7 cm long.
Fruit: Capsules borne in a spike 5 cm long.

1 — ♂ flowers,
2 — ♀ flowers,
3 — leaves and fruits, 4 — bole

Common Walnut

Juglandaceae

Juglans regia L.

The centre of the walnut's natural range is in central Asia, from where it extended as far as the Balkan Peninsula. It was cultivated by the Greeks and Romans, the boundary of its distribution shifting markedly northward. Today it is widely planted in western and central Europe, the U.S.A. and other countries. It is a tree which in central Europe does best on sheltered slopes in warm, hill country. On limestone rock it grows up to elevations of 700 to 800 metres.

A light-demanding species, the walnut requires fertile soil, and, in severe winters can suffer from frost damage. The young tree has a taproot, but in old trees the root system spreads to a distance of 15 metres from the trunk. The bark is ash-grey with shallow fissures. Open-grown trees have a short trunk and spreading crown. Under ideal conditions it can attain 30 metres in height. As in all walnuts the pith of the twigs forms plates and partitions with air spaces in between.

The tree is cultivated in gardens and avenues for its fruit — nuts — which it begins to bear from about its tenth year. The green husks split in September and October to release the nuts, whose oily kernel is very tasty and nourishing. The high quality wood (the heartwood is brownish, the sapwood greyish) is used to make furniture, rifle stocks and other special articles.

Leaves: 20—35 cm long, odd-pinnate, composed of 5—9 leaflets with entire margins, the terminal leaflet being the longest.
Flowers: Male in catkins 5—15 cm long, female in 1—4 flowered spikes, each with two stigmas.
Fruit: Ovoid drupe with nut encased in a fleshy husk.

1 — ♂ and ♀ flowers, 2 — buds, 3 — leaves and fruit, 4 — nut, 5 — seed (kernel)

Black Walnut

Juglandaceae

Juglans nigra L.

The black walnut is a native of eastern North America, where it grows alongside large rivers as far north as the Canadian border. It is a large tree attaining heights of 30 to 40 metres. Under forest competition it develops a tall, clear bole; the open-grown form has a short bole and broad crown. The bark is grey-black and deeply furrowed. The pith of the twigs contains air spaces. The leaves are alternate, odd-pinnate, the largest leaflets located in the centre. The male flowers are in drooping catkins 8 to 10 cm long, the female flowers terminal, in clusters of two to five, ripening in the autumn into a plum-like fruit with a brownish-green, semi-fleshy husk and a brown corrugated nut. The whole fruit, including the husk, falls in October; the seed is relatively small and very hard.

The black walnut was introduced into Europe in 1629. It is cultivated there as a forest tree for its high quality wood. It is more resistant to frost than the common walnut, but thrives best in the warmer regions of Europe on fertile, lowland soils with a high water table. It is a light-demanding species. The wood is used to make furniture and rifle stocks, and oil is pressed from the seeds.

Leaves: 25—50 cm long, odd-pinnate, composed of 12—23 ovate lanceolate leaflets with acute apex.
Fruit: Globose drupe, 4—5 cm long, nut with thick, brown, corrugated shell.

1 — ♂ and ♀ flowers, 2 — buds, 3 — leaf, 4 — fruit, 5 — nut, 6 — wood

Butternut

Juglandaceae

Juglans cinerea L.

The butternut is indigenous to North America, growing in the eastern part from the 35th parallel northwards to Canada. It occurs in mixed, broad-leaved woods, alongside rivers and in hill country, on deep, fertile soils, attaining heights of up to 30 metres. The bark is grey, divided by shallower fissures than those of the black walnut. The twigs and buds are grey, sticky-pubescent, and the pith of the twigs contains air spaces. The male flowers resemble those of the black walnut, the female flowers are borne in a stalked spike. The fruit is an ovoid, pointed drupe, 4 to 5 cm long, attached by a stalk approximately 10 cm long. When ripe, it falls from the tree in its entirety, including the yellowish green, sticky-pubescent husk. The nut is sweet and oily.

The butternut is resistant to frost and requires less fertile and moist soils than the black walnut. However, as it grows more slowly and the wood is not of high quality, it is cultivated in Europe mainly as an ornamental specimen tree in parks and gardens.

Leaves: 40—70 cm long, odd-pinnate, composed of 11—13 ovate leaflets; the rachis and underside of the leaflets are glandular pubescent.
Flovers: Female borne in spikes of 5—8.
Fruit: Ovoid nuts in clusters of 3—6; nut shell deeply corrugated.

1 — buds
2 — ♀ and ♂ flowers,
3 — leaf,
4 — fruit, 5 — nut

Silver Birch

Betula pendula ROTH (Syn. *B. alba* L. and *B. verrucosa* EHRH.)

Betulaceae

The birch is a tree of the northern hemisphere and its several species are distributed throughout Europe, America and Asia. Most common on the Continent is the silver birch growing in the wild from Italy to the Balkan Peninsula, northwards beyond the Arctic Circle and eastwards far into Siberia. In central Europe it is plentiful from lowland to foothill elevations.

It attains heights of 20 to 25 metres and develops a slim bole topped with a crown of slender, pendent branches. It has a fairly short life span, attaining an age of 100 to 200 years. The twigs are covered with waxy warts. The bark is white and smooth, becoming blackish and fissured at the base. The flowers appear in April, and the fruits mature in June, being gradually dispersed great distances by the wind until the onset of winter. This, plus the fact that the tree grows well even on poor soils, makes it an important colonist of forest clearings, pastures and fallow land. The silver birch is a light-demanding species and stands up well to both frost and the sun's heat. The white trunk and fresh green of its spring foliage make it an ornamental element in the landscape.

The hard, tough and flexible wood is used for interior woodwork, for wheels and also as fuel. The sap is used by the cosmetic industry, and the bark for dressing skins.

Leaves: Alternate, triangular ovate, 2.5—6 cm long, with double serrate margins.
Flowers: Male and female in separate catkins.
Fruit: Winged, 2 mm long, borne in 2—3 cm long catkin-like "cones" with scale-like bracts.

1 — ♂ and ♀ flowers,
2 — leaves,
3 — "cones",
4 — fruit,
4a — enlarged fruit, 5 — bract,
5a — enlarged bract, 6 — bark

Common Alder

Alnus glutinosa (L.) GAERTN.

The common alder is widespread throughout most of Europe, extending from Spain to Scandinavia and eastward far into Siberia. It tolerates very moist soils, and is found mainly on the banks of rivers, beside brooks and ponds, and in swampy situations. It is most plentiful in the lowlands, occurring in the mountains up to elevations of about 700 metres. It attains heights up to 30 metres, sometimes more, and develops a straight bole with black-brown bark breaking up into plates. It is easily recognized in winter by the narrowly ovoid, stalked, violet-brown buds. The broad obovate leaves are sticky in spring. The flowers, arranged in catkins, are already formed by the autumn and open in early spring (March), the female ones developing by autumn into woody cones with small winged nutlets. These are equipped with buoyant tissues that enable them to be carried great distances by air or water. The common alder is marked by the vigorous production of stump sprouts and is often grown for coppicing. The roots have small nodules with nitrogen-fixing bacteria which thereby enrich the soil. The common alder is a fairly light-demanding, fast-growing tree. The yellowish-red wood is used for the foundations of bridges, for plywood and for matches.

Leaves: Obovate to orbicular, 5—9 cm long, bluntly truncated to notched at the tip.
Flowers: Male catkins yellow, female catkins ovoid, carmine.
Fruit: Winged nutlets 3 mm long, borne in woody cones 14—18 (28) mm long.

1 — ♂ and ♀ flowers,
2 — leaves and strobiles,
3 — samara,
4 — habit

♀

♂

1

2

3

4

Grey Alder

Betulaceae

Alnus incana (L.) MOENCH.

The grey alder is primarily a tree of northern Europe. In central and southern Europe it grows in the mountains, mainly in the region of the Alps and Carpathians. It attains a height of only 15 to 20 metres and has smooth grey bark even in old age, its life span being a maximum of 60 to 100 years. The flowers appear in spring about fourteen days before those of the black poplar, the cones and seeds maturing in late September. The seed is light brown with a broad, encircling wing. The grey alder has a shallow root system, and is marked not only by vigorous production of stump suckers, but also by root suckers, especially in the northern parts of its range.

The grey alder is a light-demanding, fast-growing tree that is very tolerant and grows well on poorer soils. In central Europe, it is a colonist of alluvial land alongside mountain brooks and streams, occurring at elevations up to 1500 metres. However, it does not require moist soil, and is a colonist of screes and shallow stony slopes. It is sometimes used for afforestation on non-fertile soils which it enriches by means of its nitrogen-fixing nodules. The wood resembles that of the common alder, but is somewhat paler and of little value.

Leaves: Alternate, 3—10 cm long, ovate, with acute apex and doubly serrate margin, grey-green on the undersurface.
Fruit: Woody cones on thick stalks, nutlets pale brown, 3 mm long, with broad, encircling wing.

1 — ♂ and ♀ flowers,
2 — leaves and cones,
3 — mature cone,
4 — nutlet,
5 — bark

1

♀

♂

2

4

3

5

Common Hornbeam

Carpinus betulus L.

Betulaceae

The common hornbeam is a native of western, central and southern Europe, extending eastward as far as western Russia and the Ukraine. It requires a warm climate for good growth, and occurs only at elevations up to 600 metres. It grows in mixed stands with oak, and in some areas beech, and is also a common tree in scree forests. It reaches heights of up to 20 metres or more and often has a fluted and crooked trunk. The bark is smooth and greenish-grey, even in old trees. The buds, unlike those of the beech, are 10 mm long at the most, and pressed close to the twig. The leaves are alternate. The male and female catkins appear in May after the leaves, the fruit matures in late September. The seed does not germinate till the spring of the second year after sowing. The hornbeam is a prolific seeder and is marked by vigorous, natural regeneration.

A shade-loving tree, it makes moderate demands on soil fertility and moisture. It has a shallow, widespreading root system and is marked by the production of stump sprouts when cut back. Because it stands up well to cutting back and has dense foliage, it has been much used in landscape gardening, mainly as tall hedges and for topiary. The wood is heavy and hard, and is used for tools and building constructions.

Leaves: Narrowly oblong, pointed, 3—11 cm long by 3—5 cm wide, rounded at the base, with doubly serrate margin. *Flowers:* Male and female catkins are borne on the same tree. *Fruit:* A flat, ribbed nutlet about 8 mm long, subtended and attached to a three-lobed wing-like bract.

1 — ♂ and ♀ flowers,
2 — buds,
3 — leaves and fruits, 4 — fruit (nutlet),
5 — cross section of trunk,
6 — bark

Common Beech

Fagaceae

Fagus sylvatica L.

The common beech is widespread in western, central and southern Europe, but absent in the northern and eastern parts with severe winters. In the mountains, it occurs even at elevations above 1000 metres. It is a shade-tolerant and vigorous tree that frequently grows in pure stands, but also occurs in mixed stands together with the spruce and fir, and, at lower altitudes, with the oak, hornbeam, and other broad-leaved trees. It attains a height of 30 to 40 metres and develops a long, smooth, silver-grey trunk with a high broad crown. The pointed buds are elongate, measuring 15 to 20 mm in length, and stand away from the twig. The leaves are alternate. Beech woods are a lovely sight, in spring with their fresh green foliage, and in autumn when the leaves have turned a golden bronze. The male and female flowers appear in May, the seeds — polished red-brown nuts — mature in October, dropping to the ground, where they are eaten by forest animals. In former times pigs were herded into beech woods to feed on the nuts. The beech is a slow-growing tree whose fallen leaves enrich the soil and in certain areas it is marked by abundant natural propagation by seed. The hard wood is used to make furniture, parquet flooring, sleepers and cellulose. Its ornamental forms are often planted in parks.

Leaves: Ovate, 5—10 cm long, with entire to sinuate margin.
Flowers: Male in globose, stalked heads, female in two-flowered spike surrounded by an involucre.
Fruit: 1-cm-long nut, triangular in cross section, borne in pairs within a woody, spiny cupule which splits into 4 segments.

1 — ♂ and ♀ flowers, 2 — buds, 3 — leaves and fruits, 4 — split cupule, 5 — nut, 6 — bark

Spanish Chestnut

Fagaceae

Castanea sativa MILL.

The Spanish chestnut is indigenous to southern Europe, Asia Minor and North Africa. As early as Roman times, however, it was introduced into more northerly regions, and later it was cultivated in monastery gardens by monks. Today, centuries-old specimens may be found in Great Britain and the whole of western and central Europe. The Spanish chestnut is often a large tree attaining a height of up to 30 metres with a trunk more than two metres in diameter. The oblong-lanceolate, boldly toothed leaves are ornamental. The flowers of both sexes are borne in 10-to 20-centimetre-long, upright catkins, the male flowers in the upper part and female flowers in the lower part. They appear in late June-July and, by autumn, the female flowers develop into spiny burs bearing brownish nuts that are shed during October. The nuts, which are very tasty, are used by confectioners and also eaten roasted. The tree requires a mild climate and adequate moisture for good growth and a good nut harvest. It is sensitive to late spring and early autumn frosts, is intolerant of lime, and under forest conditions does well even in moderate shade. The high quality, durable wood is used to make furniture, barrels, fencing and also provides tannin.

Leaves: Alternate, leathery, oblong-lanceolate, 10—20 cm long, with serrate and bristle-tipped margins.
Flowers: Greenish-white, borne in upright catkins.
Fruit: Brownish nut, measuring 2—3 cm, nearly flat on one side, borne 2 or 3 in each sharply spiny bur.

1 — leaves and flowers, 2 — buds, 3 — split bur, 4 — seed (chestnut)

♀

♂

1

2

3

4

Common Oak

Quercus robur L.

The common oak is one of the most important and most widely distributed of European broad-leaved trees. Its range extends from Spain eastwards as far as the Ukraine and northwards as far as Sweden. It grows to an age of 600 to 800 years and, in the open, develops a huge trunk and broad crown. Under ideal conditions, heights of 40 metres can be attained. Up to about 20 to 30 years of age the bark is smooth and grey, in older trees it tends to become blackish-grey and deeply furrowed. The leaves are alternate with a lobed margin. The male flowers are in yellowish, slender, pendent catkins about 3 to 8 (10) centimetres long, the tiny globular female flowers are grouped in clusters of two to three on erect stalks one to three centimetres long; they appear at the beginning of May. The fruit, or acorn, is a brown elliptical nut sometimes with darker longitudinal stripes, borne in a cup on a long stalk.

The common oak grows mainly in moist bottomlands; it is the principal tree of lowland forests, where it occurs together with the elm, ash, hornbeam and lime. It grows at elevations up to 500 metres, provided that there is adequate moisture. It has a vast and deep root system and produces vigorous stump suckers when felled. The heavy, hard wood is used to make furniture, parquet flooring, barrels, boats, and other articles.

Leaves: 5—12 cm long, obovate, with 3—5 lobes on either side and eared lobes at the base. Stalk up to 1 cm long. *Flowers:* Female on stalks, male in pendent catkins. *Fruit:* Acorn, measuring 1.5—3 cm, on a stalk 1—3 cm long.

1 — ♂ and ♀ flowers, 2 — buds, 3 — leaves and fruits, 4 — acorn cut in half, 5 — cup or cupule, 6 — habit

Sessile Oak or Durmast Oak

Fagaceae

Quercus petraea LIEBL.

Much like the common oak, the durmast oak tends to be somewhat smaller with a narrower crown. It has a similar range, but does not extend as far east to regions with severe winters. Unlike the common oak it is a tree of the hills and is found at elevations up to 700 metres. It does not require soil as rich as the common oak, and even tolerates stony, acid soils. However, it requires plenty of light to thrive well. The durmast oak reaches a height of 30 to 40 metres, and its trunk is straighter than, but not as thick as, that of the common oak. The flowers, appearing 10 to 14 days later than those of the common oak, resemble them, but the female flowers, unlike those of its relative, are pressed close to the twig. The mature acorns are borne on very short stalks close to the twig. They are usually smaller, and lack the longitudinal stripes when freshly shed. The durmast oak does not begin bearing fruit until a fairly advanced age, about 40 to 60 years. It grows in mixed stands with the hornbeam and beech, in poorer and more acidic soils together with the pine and birch, and on dry, warm slopes in the company of the service tree, common or field maple, and other sun-loving woody plants. The wood is of similar quality, and has the same uses, as that of the common oak.

Leaves: Obovate, lobed, with 4—6 lobes on either side and a tapered base, stalk 1—2.5 cm long.
Flowers: Male in pendent catkins, female with a very short stalk.
Fruit: Acorns, in clusters of 2—5, broadest in the lower half, on a very short stalk.

1 — ♂ and ♀ flowers,
2 — leaves and fruits, 3 — acorn,
4 — wood

♀

♂

1

2

3

4

Turkey Oak

Fagaceae

Quercus cerris L.

The Turkey oak is a native of southern Europe, where it grows south of the Alps and Carpathians. It reaches a height of 25 to 35 metres and has a thick, deeply furrowed blackish-brown bark. In winter, it is easily distinguished by its bristle-like stipules, about 1- to 2-centimetre-long, encircling the buds on the twig. The leaves are leathery and lobed, but exhibit marked variation. The lobes are pointed. The flowers appear in May, and the fruit takes two years to mature. One-year acorns are smaller than a pea, mature acorns are larger than those of the common oak. The Turkey oak attains an age of 200 years, and in western and central Europe is cultivated in parks as an ornamental. Because of its southern origin, it is sensitive to the frost of more northerly regions, resulting in wood-checking and the formation of frost-ribs on the trunk in severe winters, which markedly decreases the value of the wood. The Turkey oak has moderate requirements as to soil properties and moisture, but does not tolerate lime-rich soils; therefore, we find the species *Quercus pubescens* Willd. growing in limestone situations in southern Europe. The wood, with red heartwood, is of poorer quality, and is used to make sleepers and mine timbers, and as fuel.

Leaves: 7—12 cm long, leathery, with 7—8 pairs of pointed lobes, lustrous, dark green above, paler green below.
Flowers: 1—5, tiny, female in very short stemmed spikes; male in sparse pendent catkins 5—8 cm long.
Fruit: Acorns measuring 2—3 cm, one-third enclosed in a scaly cupule.

1 — ♂ and ♀ flowers, 2 — buds, 3 — leaves and fruits, 4 — acorn, 5 — bark

Red Oak

Fagaceae

Quercus borealis (Syn. *Q. rubra*) L.

The red oak is a native of North America, where it grows in mixed stands, with other broad-leaved woody plants, from the 35th parallel northward to Canada. It is a robust tree, reaching a height of 35 metres. When grown in the open, it develops a broad crown with strong branches. The bark remains smooth and grey-green until an advanced age. The lobed leaves turn dark red in autumn, hence its name. The acorns mature in the autumn of the second year. They are not as popular a food with forest animals as other acorns, because of the sharp point at their tip.

The red oak grows faster than European oaks when young, and gives greater yields of timber per hectare. It has more moderate requirements as to soil conditions and grows well on acid soils, but should not be planted in water-logged soils. Because of its characteristics, it is sometimes planted in Europe for forestry purposes and is also a very popular ornamental for parks and gardens. It is more shade-tolerant than European oaks. The timber is heavy, with red-brown heartwood, and is used for the same purpose as European oaks, though its quality is not as good.

Leaves: 10—25 cm long, with 4—5 pairs of sharply toothed lobes and a broadly triangular base. *Fruit:* Reddish brown, broadly barrel-shaped acorns, 1.5—2.5 cm long, with truncate base, enclosed in a shallow cup.

1 — ♂ and ♀ flowers, one-year fruit, 2 — leaves, 3 — mature fruit, 4 — acorn, 5 — cup

Wych Elm or Scotch Elm

Ulmaceae

Ulmus glabra HUDS. (Syn. *U. montana* STOKES and *U. scabra* MILL.)

The wych elm is distributed throughout most of Europe, from Spain northward to the 65th parallel, and eastward as far as the Urals. It is found both in lowland country and high up in the mountains, even above the 1000 metre mark, most frequently in moist ravines, alongside streams and in scree woods with rich soil. The wych elm is a robust tree growing up to a height of 40 metres and developing a long, cylindrical bole topped by a rounded crown. The bark is ridged with shallow longitudinal furrows. In winter, one may observe on the twigs not only leaf buds but also globular flower buds. The flowers appear in February and March before the leaves, and, by early June, the tree sheds its ripe fruit — orbicular samaras with large membranous wings. The leaves are broadly obovate with an unequal base. Some of the leaves on young vigorous shoots may have a three-pointed tip.

The wych elm is a tree that requires partial shade, and is marked by rich natural reproduction from seed, as well as a good growth of stump suckers. At lower elevations, it is often attacked by a fungus disease that causes branches to die out. The medium heavy timber, with brownish heartwood, is used to make furniture, waggons, rifle stocks and other products.

Leaves: Slightly unequal at the base, 8—15 cm long, sometimes three-pointed at the tip, rough on the upper surface, with doubly serrate margin.
Fruit: Flat rounded-winged samara 2 cm long, with a central seed.

1 — flowers,
2 — buds,
3 — maturing fruits,
4 — ripe fruits,
5 — leaf,
6 — habit

Smooth-leaved Elm

Ulmus carpinifolia GLED.

The smooth-leaved elm is a more warmth-loving species than the wych elm and is found in Europe only as far north as the Baltic Sea. It grows mainly in the lowlands on alluvial deposits in mixed woods, together with oak, alder and poplar. It reaches a height of 30 metres, and may attain an age of several hundred years, growing a thick trunk. The globular flower buds can already be distinguished in winter. The flowers appear in February and March and the fruits — orbicular-winged samaras with a single seed — mature at the end of May. The leaves are ovate, opposite, broadest in the mid-section and with a more or less unequal base. The root system is heart-shaped with numerous, flat lateral roots. The smooth-leaved elm is marked by a vigorous production of stump suckers, and, sometimes, root suckers. It requires rich, moist soil. Found in drier situations is the form *Ulmus carpinifolia suberosa* that has corky winged plates on the branchlets. In the past several decades, the smooth-leaved elm has been greatly decimated by the Dutch elm disease, a disease caused by a fungus that causes wilting of the foliage and drying out of branches, and makes its further planting a controversial problem.

Leaves: 5—10 cm long, ovate, with markedly unequal base, smooth, dark green above, with doubly serrate margin.
Fruit: Flat, rounded-winged samara, 1—1.5 cm long, with a central seed.

1 — flowers,
2 — corky-winged twig, 3 — leaves,
4 — fruit

European White Elm

Ulmus laevis PALL.

Ulmaceae

The European white elm grows mainly in central and eastern Europe, extending west only as far as western France and not reaching Britain. It is most plentiful in lowlands on alluvial deposits, and occurs only up to heights of about 500 metres. It tolerates greater moisture than any other elm, and is not harmed even by passing floods. For that reason, it is often found on the banks of rivers, in the company of alder, poplar and willow. It is rarely found in dry situations, where it has a very brief life span.

The European white elm reaches a height of 20 to 30 metres, and is distinguished by plentiful trunk suckers. The bark is scaly, and shallowly furrowed. The buds are sharply pointed with two-toned brown scales edged with a paler hue. The flowers appear about two weeks later than those of the wych elm and are similarly borne on stalks 2 centimetres long. The ovate leaves have 14 to 20 pairs of secondary veins. Of all the European elms this species has the greatest resistance to fungus disease. The timber, with pale-brown heartwood, is not as highly prized as that of the smooth-leaved elm, and so this tree is hardly ever planted for forestry purposes.

Leaves: 5—9 cm long, ovate, with unequal base, smooth upper surface and coarsely, doubly serrate margin.
Flowers: Shortly stalked, pendent.
Fruit: Long-stalked, oval-winged samara, 1 cm long, with a central seed.

1 — flowers,
2 — buds,
3 — maturing fruits,
4 — ripe fruits,
5 — leaf

Wild Pear

Rosaceae

Pyrus communis L.

The wild pear is one of the species that have given rise to the many garden varieties cultivated for their sweet, succulent fruit. It is a native of southern, central and western Europe, but, since ancient times, has been cultivated in the vicinity of human habitations. A comparatively small tree, it grows to a height of 10 to 20 metres, and develops a dome-like crown with erect branches and thorny twigs. The bark is furrowed in squares. The alternate leaves have a stalk almost as long as the blade. The abundantly borne white flowers appear in April and early May. The rounded fruit is borne on long stalks, and is yellow-green when ripe. The wild pear has deep roots and favours light, deep soils. It needs a warmer climate than the apple, and usually grows on the margins of forests and on sun-warmed slopes up to an elevation of 400 to 500 metres. It may attain an age of 200 to 250 years. The wood is hard, fine-grained with a pink tinge, and is used to make furniture. The fruit is eaten by birds and forest animals. The leaves of some trees turn bright red in autumn.

Leaves: Round-ovate, 2—5 cm long, with a finely serrate margin and long stalks.
Flowers: White with red-purple anthers.
Fruit: 2—4 cm long, round to oval, yellow-green, long-stalked.
Seed: Black, drop-shaped.

1 — flowers,
2 — buds,
3 — leaves and fruit, 4 — flowers of cultivated variety, 5 — fruit of cultivated variety, 6 — bark

Crab Apple

Malus sylvestris MILL.

Rosaceae

The crab apple is a Eurasian species, south-east Europe being the chief centre of its distribution. It is much more frost-resistant than the pear and grows farther north. In central Europe, it occurs in hill country in mixed, broad-leaved woods, mostly in stands of oaks, where it has ample light, even near the forest floor.

The crab apple is a small tree growing to a height of only 5 to 10 metres. It has a broad crown and grey-brown bark that peels off in thin scales. The flowers, borne in clusters, are usually pinkish outside, white inside, with yellow stamens, and open one to several weeks later than those of the pear. The fruit is a small greenish yellow apple, sometimes flushed red, with a short stalk and brown, drop-like seeds.

The crab apple thrives best in moist fertile soils, and requires ample light for good growth. It is the main species, and has given rise to many cultivated varieties. Fruit-growers to this day use it as a frost-resistant dwarfing rootstock for grafting the garden varieties. In the wild, its fruit is eaten by forest animals, and many of its lovely, richly coloured, flowering forms are frequently planted in parks as ornamentals.

Leaves: Broadly ovate, 3—5 cm long, with serrate margins, 4—5 pairs of secondary veins, and stalks shorter than the blade.
Flowers: White, often flushed pink with yellow stamens.
Fruit: Yellow-green and red apple measuring 2—5 cm across.

1 — flowers,
2 — leaves and fruit, 3 — fruit of cultivated varieties,
4 — seed

Mountain Ash or Rowan

Sorbus aucuparia L.

Rosaceae

The mountain ash grows in western and central Europe from lowland to high mountain elevations up to the tree line, and, in northern Europe, even beyond the Arctic Circle. It is resistant to frost, thrives on poorer soils and is important as a pioneer tree which, because it is distributed by birds, quickly covers burned and logged areas. It reaches a height of only 15 to 20 metres. The bark is smooth and grey-brown, the buds are elongate, dark brown with greyish hairs. The white flowers appear in May, developing by autumn into bright red berries the size of a pea, which are a great favourite of birds. The tree's Latin name *aucuparia* — *avis capere* indicates that the berries were used by bird-catchers to bait their traps. The mountain ash also has a cultivated variety with larger, sweet fruit, *S. a. edulius* (syn. *dulcis*), grown in northern or mountainous regions for their fruit, which is used to make compotes, jams and spirituous drinks.

The mountain ash, and its several cultivated varieties, is also popular for planting alongside roads as an ornamental for its spring flowers and bright autumn coloration. The wood has little durability.

Leaves: Alternate, odd-pinnate, 10—25 cm long, with usually 6—7 pairs of elliptical, sharply serrate leaflets 3—5 cm long.
Flowers: Creamy white in dense clusters.
Fruit: Bright red berries with drop-like, 4-mm-long seeds.

1 — flowers,
2 — buds,
3 — leaves and fruits, 4 — fruit

Whitebeam

Rosaceae

Sorbus aria CRANTZ.

The whitebeam is widespread in southern, central and western Europe, including Great Britain, the southern tip of Sweden marking the northernmost limit of its range. Throughout this area, however, it occurs fairly sparsely. A light-demanding and warmth-loving species, it is often found growing on chalk or limestone hills facing south. In such conditions, it may be found at elevations even over 1000 metres.

The whitebeam is a small tree, 10 to 15 metres high, often occurring only as a shrub on shallow soils. The bark is grey-brown, the ovoid buds are green and slightly downy. The leaves have no resemblance to those of the mountain ash, being ovate in outline and densely white hairy beneath. The white flowers, borne in broad panicles, appear from May to June. The berry-like fruit is broadly ovoid and scarlet. The stalk and remainder of the calyx are covered with whitish down. It is an important tree in the afforestation of karst areas and is a popular ornamental in city parks and gardens. Growing in the high mountain alpine zone is the shrub form *Sorbus chamaemespilus* Crantz., with leaves that are hairless below.

Leaves: 5—12 cm long, elliptic to broadly ovate, bluntly pointed, lustrous green above, white tomentose below, with doubly serrate margin. *Flowers:* White. *Fruit:* Berry-like, scarlet, 8—15 mm long.

1 — flower,
2 — buds,
3 — leaves and fruits, 4 — fruit cut in two halves

Wild Service Tree

Rosaceae

Sorbus torminalis CRANTZ.

The wild service tree has a similar range to that of the whitebeam, though it does not extend as far north and east. It requires a mild climate and thus is found in hilly country only up to 500 metres. Ideal conditions are provided by limestone soils and sun-facing slopes, though in Britain it is often found on clay soils.

The wild service tree reaches a height of 20 to 25 metres and because it may live 200 to 300 years, one may come across the occasional, robust specimen with a vast broad crown. The bark is furrowed in squares, the buds are spherical, lustrous yellow-green. The leaves may take on red tints in autumn. The white flowers are borne in erect panicles 6 to 8 centimetres across. The brown fruits are edible following the first frost. The wild service tree has a heart-shaped root system with long lateral roots, and reproduces also by root suckers. The wood is heavy and very hard, and is used for woodcarvings and making rulers, gauges and instrument components. An ornamental tree, it is also suitable for planting alongside roads and in tree avenues.

In southern Europe it often hybridizes with the whitebeam to produce the hybrid broad-leaved whitebeam (*Sorbus latifolia* Pers.)

Buds: Spherical, yellow-green.
Leaves: 7—12 cm long, with 5 to 7 lobes, the basal pair growing out horizontally, and a serrate margin.
Flowers: White.
Fruit: Berry-like, brown, ovoid, 10—12 mm long, covered with small pale dots.

1 — flowers,
2 — buds,
3 — leaves and fruits, 4 — fruit

Service Tree

Sorbus domestica L.

The service tree grows in North Africa, Asia Minor and southern Europe, as far north as central Germany. It is sensitive to frost, and requires a mild climate and a fertile, mineral-rich soil to grow well. A slow-growing tree, it reaches a height of 10 to 15 metres, but because it may attain an age of 500 to 600 years one occasionally sees a tree that is 20 metres high. Unlike the mountain ash, the reddish brown bark is longitudinally fissured, even in the young tree. The leaves, odd-pinnate, and grey-downy beneath until midsummer, appear about 14 days later than in the mountain ash. The service tree begins to bear flowers and fruit at the age of 25 to 35 years, sometimes sooner. The flowers, white, sometimes tinged with pink, are larger than those of the mountain ash and the fruits are reddish-yellow and pear-shaped. At one time, the service tree was grown in gardens and orchards, but today its fruits are eaten only by birds and animals. In warmer climates, it is used as an ornamental and planted alongside roads and in parks. The timber, with red-brown heartwood, is very hard, and is used to make wheels and in joinery.

Leaves: 15—18 cm long, odd-pinnate, with 5—9 pairs of lanceolate, serrate leaflets.
Flowers: White to pinkish, in panicles.
Fruit: Small, pear-shaped, sometimes ovoid, brownish or greenish, often flushed reddish-yellow, 2—3 cm long, with 2—4 seeds.

1 — flowers,
2 — leaves and fruits

Wild Cherry or Gean

Prunus avium L.

For centuries, the wild cherry has been cultivated in gardens and its seeds distributed by birds, so that now it is difficult to determine its original, natural area of distribution. Today, it is found growing in mixed, broad-leaved woods throughout western, central and eastern Europe, in lowland, hilly and sub-alpine areas up to heights of 700 to 900 metres. It is a robust tree which, under forest competition, attains a height of 20 to 25 metres and develops a tall, straight bole. Grown in the open it forms a short trunk and broad crown. The smooth, red-brown bark becomes shallowly fissured in older trees. The buds are ovoid; flower buds are plumper and borne in clusters on the side branches. The white, long-stalked flowers open in April and early May, developing into dark red drupes which ripen at the beginning of July. These are a favourite of birds, which disperse the seeds throughout the surrounding countryside. The red-brown wood is of high quality and is used to make furniture and in joinery. All cultivated forms of sweet cherry are descended from this species.

Leaves: 6—15 cm long, obovate, with roughly serrate margins and a slender point; there are 2 reddish glands on the stalk.
Flowers: White.
Fruit: Dark red drupe, 1 cm long, with long stalk and smooth stone.

1 — flowers,
2 — buds,
3 — leaves and fruits,
4 — cultivated variety

Mahaleb Cherry

Prunus mahaleb L.

The mahaleb cherry is a native of southern Europe and south-western Asia. It requires a mild climate but is tolerant of soil conditions, and can grow on dry and stony slopes in hilly country. It is found in oak woods and in the company of shrubs, especially on limestone soils. It is a small tree, reaching a height of only 6 to 10 metres, and frequently occurs in shrub form. The trunk is generally crooked, and the crown has pendent branches. The shoots are thin, the buds small and ovoid. The white flowers, borne in a loose, upright raceme, appear about a week later than those of the bird cherry. The fruit is a black, spherical ovoid drupe, ripening in late July, with a small smooth stone.

The mahaleb cherry is used as a pioneer in the afforestation of warm karst areas. It is sometimes cultivated as a short rotation crop for the making of pipes, cigarette holders and other articles of turnery. In dry and warm areas it is a good tree for parks and roadsides. Fruit growers use it as a rootstock for grafting cultivated varieties.

Leaves: Alternate, 3—7 cm long, broadly ovate, pointed, lustrous green above, with serrate margins; stalk glandular or without glands.
Flowers: White and fragrant, 1—1.5 cm across.
Fruit: Drupes the size of a pea, black and bitter, borne in a loose, upright raceme.

1 — flowers,
2 — leaves and fruits

Bird Cherry

Prunus padus L.

The bird cherry is distributed throughout most of Europe, extending northward as far as central Sweden and eastward to the Yenisei River. It grows mainly in moist situations alongside lakes and ponds and on alluvial deposits; alongside streams, it may be found at elevations over 1000 metres. The bird cherry is a small tree 5 to 15 metres high, with a broad crown and pendent branches. The bark is grey-black, thin, and covered with small warts. When peeled from the twig it gives off an unpleasant scent reminiscent of bitter almonds — a characteristic of this species. The fragrant white flowers in pendent racemes open in May. They are succeeded in July by black, astringent drupes which are eaten by birds.

The bird cherry requires partial shade, and often forms the lower stratum of damp woods. It requires comparatively rich and moist soil to grow really well. The wood is of good quality but of little importance because of the tree's small size.

Cultivated locally for its wood in European forests and as an ornamental in parks is the North American black cherry (*Prunus serotina* Ehr.), which grows to a height of 25 metres and has scaly bark. It is more tolerant of soil and climatic conditions.

Leaves: Alternate, lustrous green, elliptic or obovate and slender pointed, 6—12 cm long, with fine, sharply serrate margins and stalks with 1 to 2 glands. *Fruit:* Ovoid black drupe, 6—8 mm long, borne in loose racemes, with furrowed stone.

1 — flowers,
2 — buds,
3 — leaves and fruits, 4 — fruit and stone,
5 — twig of black cherry

Tulip Tree

Magnoliaceae

Liriodendron tulipifera L.

The tulip tree's name is derived from the shape of the flowers which somewhat resemble those of a tulip. It is a native of North America, where it grows from the Canadian border southward as far as Arkansas and Florida. It is found chiefly in moist forests on rich alluvial soils. Fossil remains of leaves indicate that, before the Ice Age, it or a similar species was also widely distributed in Europe.

The tulip tree is a large tree, growing, in Europe, to a height of 30 to 35 metres, and developing a straight trunk with roughly furrowed bark. It attains an age of 400 to 500 years. In winter it is distinguished by its distinctive buds and large leaf scars, in summer by its ornamental and striking saddle-shaped leaves. The flowers, appearing in June, are roughly tulip-shaped, 4 to 5 centimetres long. The winged seeds form a cone-like structure and disintegrate in the spring of the following year.

The tulip tree is widely cultivated in the parks of western and central Europe for its ornamental flowers, and for its leaves that turn yellow in autumn. The light wood, with yellow-brown heartwood and pale sapwood, is used to make veneers and musical instruments.

Leaves: Alternate, 10—15 cm long, with 2—4 lobes, entire margins and long stalks. *Flowers:* With yellow-green sepals and orange flushed petals. *Fruit:* Cone-like, 5—8 cm long, composed of winged seeds.

1 — flower and leaf, 2 — buds, 3 — fruiting "cone", 4 — seed (nutlet)

White Mulberry

Moraceae

Morus alba L.

The white mulberry is a native of China, Japan and India. Its leaves serve as food for the silkworm, whose cocoon is used for the production of silk. It was introduced into Europe as early as the 7th century A.D., together with the silkworm. One hundred years and more ago it was far more widely cultivated than it is today, now that silk has been replaced by other fibres. The white mulberry is a small tree growing to a height of 10 to 15 metres and developing a broad crown. The bark is grey-brown and furrowed with longitudinal ridges. The leaves are broadly ovate, often three lobed. The tiny flowers are borne in short dense spikes, usually monoeciously, rarely dioeciously. The milky-white loganberry-like fruit has a bland, sweetish taste and matures in June.

The white mulberry requires partial shade and warm climate, Europe's wine-growing regions providing the best conditions for its growth. It is damaged by frost, but has good powers of regeneration by suckers. It is cultivated in parks as a specimen tree, and is also good in tree avenues, and for planting in hedges. At one time it was grown in gardens as a fruit tree. The related black mulberry (*Morus nigra* L.), with dark red fruits, is a native of Iran and Afghanistan.

Leaves: Alternate, broadly ovate, 6—18 cm long, often three-lobed, lustrous green above, with roughly serrate margin.
Flowers: Male and female in short dense spikes.
Fruit: A 1—2.5 cm long aggregate fruit comprising tightly packed fleshy white drupes.

1 — ♂ and ♀ flowers, 2 — buds, 3 — leaves and fruits, 4 — fruit of black mulberry

London Plane

Platanus × hispanica MUENCHH. (*P. ×
acerifolia* WILD.)

The London plane tree is a natural hybrid between
the oriental plane (*Platanus orientalis* L.), and the
American plane or buttonwood (*Platanus occidentalis*
L.), and was first recorded about 1663. It is more
resistant to frost than the parent trees and thus
widespread throughout Europe all the way to the
Baltic Sea. It is a large tree, reaching a height of
30 metres and a trunk diameter of 2 metres.
Grown in the open it develops a huge spreading
crown with thick branches and numerous strangely
crooked branchlets. The bark peels off in thin
flakes, exposing patches of pale yellow, inner bark.
The distinctive buds are conical with a single
cap-like scale. The male and female flowers, borne
in small globose heads on long stalks, appear in
May. The fruits are small downy nutlets borne in
globose heads, which disintegrate in spring.

The London plane tree requires a fair amount
of light and rich soil. It is popularly planted as an
ornamental in city parks and streets because it
tolerates the dusty and smoke-polluted atmosphere. It is also impressive as a solitary tree. The
wood is hard, with darker heartwood.

Leaves: Palmately
3—5 lobed,
sometimes
irregularly
toothed,
12—25 cm long,
the central lobe
broader at the
base than it is
long, the stalk
expanded at the
base to cover the
axillary bud.
Fruit: Cylindrical
nutlets measuring
5—6 mm and
borne in stalked
globose heads
measuring
2—3 cm.

1 — ♂ flowers,
2 — ♀ flowers,
3 — buds,
4 — leaves and
fruit heads,
5 — nutlet,
6 — bark

False Acacia or Black Locust

Leguminosae

Robinia pseudoacacia L.

The false acacia is a native of North America, where it grows in mixed broad-leaved woods from Pennsylvania to Georgia and Oklahoma. It was named after the French botanist Jean Robin, who introduced it into Europe in 1601. Today, it is widespread throughout western, central, eastern and southern Europe and in some areas is so familiar as to be mistakenly considered a native species. It reaches a height of 20 to 30 metres, the bark is deeply furrowed and the twigs thorny. The ornamental, odd-pinnate leaves appear at the end of May, and, soon after, the white, fragrant flowers, borne in pendent racemes. The false acacia has a wide-spreading root system extending far from the trunk, and nitrogen-fixing bacteria in nodules on the roots; thus it improves the soil, though at the same time it poisons it with its root excretions. The false acacia is marked by the vigorous production of stump suckers, and regeneration by root suckers. It is a fast-growing tree and requires abundant light, but otherwise will grow on poorer and drier soils. For this reason, and because of its wide-spreading root system, it is often used for erosion control on slopes, embankments and sand dunes. In warm, wine-growing regions, it is also grown in forest stands. The flowers yield a rich harvest for bees, and the wood is of good quality.

Leaves: Odd-pinnate, 10—25 cm long, composed of 3—9 pairs of elliptic leaflets with rounded tips and entire margins.
Flowers: Pea-shaped, white, borne in pendent racemes.
Fruit: Flat, brownish pod or legume, 5—11 cm long, with blackish seeds.

1 — buds,
2 — flowers,
3 — leaves and fruits, 4 — pod with seeds,
5 — wood

Honey Locust

Leguminosae

Gleditsia triacanthos L.

The honey locust was named for the botanist Gottlieb Gleditsch and for its three-branched, 5 to 15-centimetre-long spines, which grow on the trunk and branches. It is a native of eastern North America, where it is found on moist, rich soils from Texas northward to the 43rd parallel. It can tolerate drier situations, and is planted in tree belts in the prairies. The honey locust was introduced into Europe in about 1700 and is now abundant in the warm lowlands of western and southern Europe. It reaches a height of 30 to 45 metres, and has a smooth, blackish bark that peels off in large flakes. The inconspicuous greenish flowers are arranged in racemes four to seven centimetres long. The long, twisted pod remains on the tree until winter. The honey locust is a light-demanding tree and stands up well to cutting-back. It is found in parks, and sometimes in the vicinity of country dwellings, where it is used as a thorny hedge. The wood, which is hard with reddish brown heartwood, is highly prized. The unripe pods are a favourite food of livestock and the dye they yield is used in colouring fabrics.

Leaves: Alternate, even-pinnate and bipinnately compound, 12—30 cm long, with 10—15 pairs of narrow elliptic leaflets, the margin sparingly toothed.
Fruit: A reddish brown pod or legume 20—40 cm long.
Seed: Yellow-brown, 1 cm long.

1 — twig and thorns,
2 — flowers,
3 — leaf, 4 — pod,
5 — seed

Tree of Heaven

Simaroubaceae

Ailanthus altissima SWINGLE

The tree of heaven is native to the southern half of China, and in 1751 was introduced into Europe, where it is now grown in the cities and parks in the western, central and southern areas. Thriving best in a mild climate, it grows well in warm lowland areas, particularly in cities, where it has great powers of natural regeneration on dumps and demolished sites. It is a fast-growing tree that requires abundant light but it is tolerant of a wide range of soil types and stands up well to dry weather and air pollution. It flourishes in light soil and its wide-spreading root system serves to bind sandy soil. It is marked by a vigorous production of stump and root suckers. It is easily damaged by severe cold, and is not suitable for planting in locations with frosty winters.

The tree of heaven reaches a height of 20 to 25 metres, and develops a stout trunk with smooth dark grey bark. The shoots are thick, and have large leaf scars below the buds. The odd-pinnate leaves are very ornamental, and the inconspicuous yellow-green flowers, arranged in panicles, are usually borne dioeciously. The winged fruit is capable of travelling great distances. The tree of heaven is an important ornamental for city parks and avenues.

Leaves: Odd-pinnate, 30—60 cm long, consisting of 7—22 pairs of ovate, pointed leaflets that have 2—4 glandular teeth at the base. *Fruit:* Propeller-shaped samara, about 3—4 cm long, with a central rounded seed.

1 — budding twig, 2 — flowers, 3 — leaf, 4 — fruits

Sycamore

Aceraceae

Acer pseudoplatanus L.

The sycamore is the most important European species of the genus *Acer*. It is a tree of western, central and southern Europe, its northward distribution falling short of the Baltic Sea, but it is much planted elsewhere and now naturalized as far north as the Shetland Islands and southern Scandinavia. It is scattered throughout woods at elevations ranging from hill country to heights of 1500 metres, growing mainly in the mountains. Preferring a cool, humid climate and a well-drained soil, it is found predominantly in mountain valleys, scree woods and alongside mountain streams. It reaches a height of 30 to 35 metres and a trunk diameter of 150 centimetres, living for several hundred years. The bark is grey-brown, and peels off in small flat plates; the upright buds are green, the scales edged with brown. The long-stalked leaves are opposite, and the greenish flowers appear in April and May.

The sycamore has a large, spreading root system, but does not produce many stump sprouts. The hard, light-coloured wood is used to make furniture, veneers and musical instruments. The decorative wood with a curly pattern is highly prized. During the Napoleonic Wars attempts were made to produce sugar from the sap of the European maples.

Leaves: Palmate, 5—7 lobed and coarsely toothed, 7—16 cm across, grey-green below, with serrate margin; stalk does not exude milky sap when broken.
Flowers: Small, yellow-green in pendent racemes.
Fruit: Double samara with wings forming an acute angle.
Seed: Globular.

1 — buds,
2 — flowers,
3 — leaves and fruits, 4 — bark

Norway Maple

Acer platanoides L.

The Norway maple is more resistant to frost than the sycamore, and in Sweden is found as far north as latitude 64°, its distribution extending deep into areas with inland climate all the way to the Urals. It is a tree of lower and submontane elevations, and in Europe it is found at altitudes up to about 700 metres, growing mostly on rocky locations alongside streams, or on rocky slopes. It, too, is a large tree of fine proportions, reaching a height of 25 to 30 metres, but it never attains the diameter of the sycamore. It differs from the latter in having longitudinally fissured bark, reddish brown buds pressed close to the twig, and sharply-pointed, lobed leaves. When broken off, the stalk exudes a milky white sap. The bright yellow-green flowers appear in April together with the leaves, and are pollinated by insects. The double samaras have wide-spreading wings.

The Norway maple is shade-tolerant and needs rich, moist soil for good growth. The wood is very like that of the sycamore in appearance and is used for similar purposes, but is not as highly valued. The Norway maple has many ornamental forms, including purple and variegated leaved kinds. It tolerates the smoky atmosphere of cities, and is popularly planted in parks and city streets.

Leaves: Palmate, 5—7 lobed, 5—15 cm across, clefts between the leaves entire, lobes sharply pointed; stalk exudes milky liquid when broken off.
Flowers: Yellow, in erect panicles.
Fruit: Double samara with widely spreading wings and flattened seeds.

1 — buds,
2 — flowers,
3 — leaf,
4 — fruits,
5 — bark

Common or **Field Maple**

Acer campestre L.

The field maple is widespread in western, central and eastern Europe but requires a milder climate than both preceding species and does not extend northward as far as Scandinavia. Even in central Europe it is found only in warmer regions, at elevations up to about 500 metres. It generally grows to a height of no more than 7 to 15 metres. Only in riverine woods or rich soil does it attain a height of more than 15 metres. The bark is furrowed into rhombic plates and the variety *suberosa* has corky wings on the twigs. The leaf stalk exudes a milky substance when broken off. The yellow-green flowers appear at the beginning of May, together with the leaves. The fruit, a wide double samara with parallel wings, ripens in September and October.

The field maple is a slow-growing tree with a shallow root system. It produces a vigorous crop of stump suckers, and also puts out root suckers. It is generally found growing on well-drained, sun-warmed slopes amid other trees and in hedgerows. The hard wood is highly valued and used to make lathe-turned articles, in wood-carving and joinery.

Leaves: Palmate 5-lobed, 4—7(10) cm wide, fairly variable, lobes bluntly pointed, with entire or sparingly toothed margins.
Flowers: Greenish, in upright panicles.
Fruit: A double samara with flattened seeds.

1 — buds,
2 — flowers,
3 — leaves and fruits, 4 — fruit,
5 — twig with corky wings,
6 — shape (habit)

Box-elder

Acer negundo L.

The Box-elder is a native of North America, where it has a wide range of distribution, extending from California to Florida and northwards to Canada. It was introduced into Europe in 1688, and today is cultivated throughout the entire Continent, tolerating even the climate of northern Europe. In some areas it is well naturalized and appears wild. It lives to an age of only a hundred years or so and reaches a height of 10 to 20 metres. The twigs are green, covered with a bluish bloom when young. The trunk is often crooked, and the bark is divided into ridges by shallow fissures. Unlike all other European maples, it has compound odd-pinnate leaves. The tiny greenish flowers are clustered in pendent racemes and appear as the leaves unfold. The fruit, which matures in autumn, appears also in pendent clusters.

In its native environment, the Box-elder grows mostly in river valleys, and near lakes, on moist soils. However, it appears to be very adaptable, and also grows fairly well in dry situations. It is of little importance in European forestry, because of its brief life span and poor quality wood, but is often planted as an ornamental. Its rapid growth in youth makes it a good tree for providing quick screens in parks and gardens. Also very ornamental are the yellow and silver variegated leaved forms which are more frequently seen in gardens.

Leaves: 13—25 cm long, odd-pinnate, composed of 3—5 (sometimes 7 or 9) coarsely toothed leaflets, the terminal leaflet generally three-lobed.
Flowers: Unisexual in drooping long stalked clusters.
Fruit: A double samara, with wings forming an acute angle and ovoid seeds.

1 — ♂ flowers,
2 — ♀ flowers,
3 — buds,
4 — leaves and maturing fruits,
5 — fruits

♂

2 ♀

Tartarian Maple

Acer tataricum L.

Aceraceae

The Tartarian maple is widespread in southeast Europe, extending northward to southern Slovakia and eastward as far as Iran. It is widely cultivated today as an ornamental in the parks of western and central Europe, and is completely frost-resistant in this area. It branches close to the ground and has the shape of a large shrub 4 to 10 metres high. The twigs are slender and brownish, the buds small. The greenish white flowers appear at the end of May after the leaves unfurl. The samaras have red wings before maturation, but, when ripe, they turn entirely brown.

The Tartarian maple is very tolerant of dry situations, and is plentiful even in the Russian steppes. In parks, it is planted on dry slopes, and as tall green hedges in dry locations. It is also very attractive as a solitary specimen tree. The related Manchurian maple (*Acer ginnala* Maxim.), a native of the Far East, is frequently cultivated. It, too, has the shape of a shrub, but differs from the Tartarian maple in having distinctive three-lobed leaves which turn yellow or bright red in autumn.

Leaves: Palmate, opposite, ovate, 6—10 cm long, with two, slightly demarcated lobes, serrate margin and rounded base. *Fruit:* A double samara, the wings forming an acute angle and often overlapping, with an ovoid seed.

1 — flowers,
2 — leaves and maturing fruits,
3 — ripe fruits

Horse-chestnut

Hippocastanaceae

Aesculus hippocastanum L.

The horse-chestnut is one of the most attractive of trees when in flower. It is a native of western Asia and south-eastern Europe, where it occurs in broad-leaved forests in the mountains at elevations of 700 to 1200 metres. It was introduced into other parts of Europe as early as 1576, and was widely planted in parks and avenues, as well as in game preserves as food for forest animals. The horse-chestnut grows to a height of 25 metres and develops a dense, broadly ovoid crown. The trunk is often twisted, always in the right-hand direction, and the bark peels in thin plates. In winter, it is easily distinguished by robust twigs, large, sticky, red-brown opposite buds and horseshoe-shaped leaf scars. The palmately compound leaves appear in early spring and the white flowers, spotted yellow and red, appear in May, making the horse-chestnut look like a lighted Christmas tree. In autumn, the flowers are succeeded by leathery, thorny fruits about 5 centimetres long, which split to release one to two polished reddish-brown seeds or "conkers". These are often gathered by children and in the forests are a favourite food of red and roe deer.

The horse-chestnut thrives best in rich, moist soil, but is tolerant of poor light and pollution. In severe winters it can be slightly damaged by frost. The wood is not considered of much value.

Leaves: Large, palmately compound, consisting of 5—7 obovate leaflets.
Flowers: White, in upright panicles.
Fruit: Spiny capsule with 1—2 reddish-brown seeds up to 3.5 cm long.

1 — buds, 2 — flowers and leaf, 3 — splitting fruit, 4 — seed

Small-leaved Lime

Tilia cordata MILL.

The small-leaved lime is widespread throughout most of Europe, extending northwards to Sweden, and eastwards to the Urals. In western and central Europe it occurs in oak forests in lowland and hill country. It also grows as a scattered tree in riverine forests, and is plentiful in scree woods. It grows to a height of 25 to 30 metres and, under forest competition, develops a long, straight bole; open-grown forms have a short, stout trunk with large, broadly ovoid crown. It may live to an age of 500 to 800 years. Centuries-old solitary trees in the country afford not only shade and respite from the heat, but also a lovely sight for the eyes to feast on. The small-leaved lime is one of the latest-flowering trees. When the yellowish-green flowers appear in July, their heady fragrance spreads far and wide. They are visited by bees, and the tree is thus of importance for honey production. The rounded leaves have rusty hairs in the axils of the veins on the underside. The globose fruit has a smooth, thin shell. Small-leaved lime stands up well to hard pruning, and is highly prized for planting in avenues. The soft, whitish wood is used for making pencils and for woodcarvings. The bast fibres are used in gardening for tying, and for making plaited articles.

Leaves: Alternate, round-cordate, 5—8 cm long, with pointed tip and serrate margin, blue-green on the underside with rusty hairs in the axils of the veins.
Flowers: Pale yellow-green, 5—8 in a drooping cluster.
Fruit: A globular, nut-like capsule, 4—6 mm long, with one or more seeds.

1 — buds,
2 — leaves and flowers, 3 — fruit,
4 — bark

Large-leaved Lime

Tilia platyphyllos SCOP.

The large-leaved lime is closely related to the small-leaved lime, and has a similar range of distribution. However, its northern boundary does not extend to the Baltic Sea, and, in the east, it occurs only as far as the western Ukraine. It is most plentiful in hilly country and foothills at elevations of 400 to 700 metres, though the occasional, single tree may be found up to 1000 metres above sea level. It occurs in broad-leaved woods and requires richer and moister soil than the small-leaved lime.

The large-leaved lime grows to a greater height and attains greater dimensions than its relative. Specimens as much as 30 to 33 metres high are not unknown; very old, solitary trees have trunks up to 3 to 4 metres thick. It is said that the large-leaved lime may live longer than a thousand years. For this reason, it is popularly planted on hilltops, or beside isolated homesteads, monuments, or churches, and in parks and avenues. The large-leaved lime flowers some 10 to 14 days sooner than the small-leaved lime, and mixed plantings of the two species prolong the period for bee-feeding to a full month. The main characteristics that make it easy to distinguish the one from the other are the underside of the leaf, the period of flowering and the shape of the fruit. In the wild they frequently hybridize to produce the hybrid *Tilia europaea* L. (*intermedia* DC), which blends the characters of both parents.

Leaves: Cordate, 6—12 cm long, pointed and sharply toothed, paler green below with white hairs in the axils of the veins.
Fruit: An ovoid capsule measuring 8 mm, with 4—5 ribs, slightly tomentose; 2—4 nuts in a cluster, attached to the floral bract which dries and acts as a wing for seed dispersal.

1 — leaves and flowers, 2 — fruit, 3 — habit

Silver or White Lime

Tilia tomentosa MOENCH.

The silver lime is a native of south-eastern Europe, where it occurs in the Balkan Peninsula and as far east as the southern Ukraine. It is found in oak forests, and frequently on limestone hills. It has moderate requirements of soil properties and moisture, and has done very well in the parks and streets of western and central European cities; it has also proved to be far more tolerant of the dry and smoky atmosphere of the cities than the local species of lime.

The silver lime grows to a height of 25 to 30 metres, and develops a large, ovoid crown with dense foliage. The dark grey bark is smooth, even in older trees. The twigs and buds are slightly hairy and the leaves are covered with silvery-grey hairs below. The pale, yellow-green flowers appear a few days later than those of the small-leaved lime and are even more fragrant. The fruit is a rounded, downy capsule. Unlike the other European lime trees, the silver lime retains its thick green foliage until late autumn, when the leaves turn yellow. It is an attractive ornamental and often planted in parks and avenues.

Leaves: Round-cordate, pointed, 5—11 cm long, often asymmetrical, silvery-grey tomentose below, with doubly serrate margin.
Flowers: 6—10 in a pendent cluster.
Fruit: A globular, slightly ribbed capsule, 2—4 borne together attached to the floral bract which acts as a wing for dispersal by wind.

1 — buds,
2 — flowers,
3 — leaves,
4 — underside of leaf, 5 — fruit

Common Ash

Oleaceae

Fraxinus excelsior L.

The common ash is widely distributed in southern, central and western Europe, the northern boundary of its range extending from Great Britain across Scandinavia to Leningrad and the Volga River. It is most plentiful in lowland forests on alluvial river deposits, and alongside streams. It is also found growing in scree woods in hilly country and high up in the mountains, even at elevations above 1000 metres. It requires rich, moist soil to do really well and often occurs in damp gullies and near streams, though it does not tolerate water-logged situations. Despite this, the common ash is tolerant of soil and situation and, in Britain at least, it often occurs on thin limestone or chalk soils. Although shade-tolerant when young, older trees require abundant light.

The common ash reaches a height of 30 to 35 metres or more under forest conditions, and develops a slender, straight bole with high set crown. It is sensitive to late spring frosts and, when the terminal shoot is damaged, often develops twin stems. In winter, it is easily distinguished by its squat black buds, in summer by the odd-pinnate leaves. The male, female or bisexual flowers, without sepals or petals, appear before the leaves and are pollinated by the wind. The common ash is an important timber tree, and is also planted in parks and avenues. There are several ornamental cultivated varieties, notably *F.e. pendula*, with a broad crown of pendulous branches.

Leaves: 20—35 cm long, odd-pinnate, composed of 3—6 pairs of lanceolate, 6—13 cm long leaflets with serrate margins.
Flowers: Inconspicuous, borne in panicles before the leaves in April.
Fruit: A slightly twisted samara, about 3 cm long with an ellipsoid seed.

1 — buds,
2 — ♂ flowers,
3 — ♀ flowers,
4 — leaf,
5 — fruits

White Ash

Oleaceae

Fraxinus americana L.

The white ash is a native of the eastern half of North America as far as latitude 53°. It occurs in mixed, broad-leaved forests, on alluvial deposits alongside rivers and streams, and in moist forest associations. In Europe, it tolerates floods of longer duration and more water-logged soils than the common ash. It also grows on less fertile soils, and is not damaged by late spring frosts because its leaves unfold later.

The white ash reaches a height of 30 to 40 metres and the bark is more coarsely furrowed than that of the common ash. It also differs from the latter in having brown buds. The odd-pinnate leaves are composed of broader, ovate leaflets and the seeds are narrowly lanceolate, about one-half narrower than the tongue-shaped wings. The seed, unlike that of the common ash, germinates in the spring of the following year. As it grows no faster than the common ash and its wood is of poorer quality it is not cultivated in European forests, though it has some value as an ornamental specimen tree in parks and avenues, especially on the poorer soils.

Leaves: odd-pinnate, composed of 2—4 pairs of ovate leaflets measuring 6—15 cm in length with coarsely serrate margins.
Flowers: Often dioeciously borne.
Fruit: Narrow, lanceolate samara with an almost cylindrical seed and a tongue-shaped wing.

1 — buds,
2 — ♂ flowers,
3 — ♀ flowers,
4 — leaf and fruits

1 2 3 4 ♂ ♀

Manna Ash

Fraxinus ornus L.

The manna ash is a tree of south-eastern Europe, where it grows south of the Alps and Carpathians. It occurs in Spain and southern France, but the chief centre of its distribution is Italy and the Balkan Peninsula, where it is found on dry, sun-warmed slopes in oak forests. In the northern areas of its range, it occurs chiefly on limestone soils. In the mountains it may be found at elevations up to 1200 metres.

The manna ash is a small tree reaching a height of only 10 to 20 metres. The bark is grey and covered with warts, the buds are greyish violet. The flowers, unlike those of other ashes, have narrow white petals and the samaras are smaller than those of the common ash.

The manna ash thrives on well-drained soils that are exposed to strong sunlight in the summer. It is, however, tolerant of soil conditions and will grow in cooler climates. It is an important tree in the afforestation of karst areas and dry slopes devastated by grazing. In former times, the liquid "manna" (sap) yielded by the bark was used for pharmaceutical purposes in Italy. Today, however, its production is greatly limited. The attractive, fragrant flowers of this tree make it a popular ornamental in parks.

Leaves: 15—20 cm long, odd-pinnate, composed of 2—4 pairs of broadly ovate, irregularly toothed leaflets 3—7 cm long.
Flowers: Usually dioeciously borne in large panicles with 4 narrow white petals.
Fruit: A narrowly oblong samara, 2—2.5 cm long, and having a notched wing.

1 — buds,
2 — flowers,
3 — leaf and fruits

NATURAL DISTRIBUTION AND INTRODUCTION OF EXOTICS

Every plant on Earth occurs in a certain region that can be marked out on a map. This region is termed its area of natural distribution. Knowledge of these areas is of great importance, because the woody plant grows for hundreds, and even thousands, of years in the given area, and is adapted to the climatic conditions of the locality, thus making it possible to determine whether it prefers a coastal or inland, lowland or alpine climate. The study of other data reveals what temperatures it is able to withstand in winter, as well as its soil and moisture requirements.

In the individual parts of its range, where it is exposed to varying conditions, the woody plant varies in appearance as well as in certain other characteristics. This is especially true of species with a wide area of distribution, where one will find several local races, called ecotypes. Thus, for instance, the pines of northern Sweden, Finland and Lapland have long, slender, tapering crowns which are better equipped to bear the heavy load of snow usual in northern winters, and make the most of the rays of the low-lying sun. Pines from the lower, dry elevations of central Europe, on the other hand, have broad crowns to shade their site as much as possible. Similarly, mountain spruces growing at high elevations, or in cold valleys, have slender, narrow crowns. Variations in climate are also reflected in the onset of budding and in other aspects of the annual cycle of growth. Such characteristics that have developed as a result of mutations which have given an environmental advantage over a period of several generations are hereditary and passed on to the offspring.

The boundaries of the area of natural distribution, however, do not constitute a line of demarcation outside which plants would not prosper. It is necessary to realize that plants, including trees and shrubs, migrated in the wake of the retreating ice sheet in the period following the Ice Age and thus established

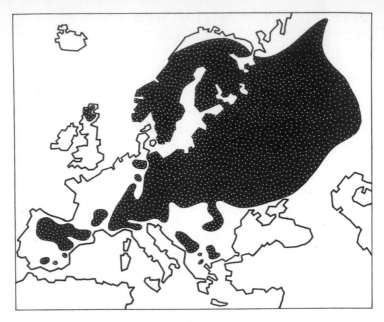

Fig. 9. Range of natural distribution: a - pine,

new ranges. Some species have not as yet occupied the whole
of the area that would suit their needs. Other species came up
against insurmountable obstacles such as mountain ranges, and
broad river valleys, though beyond these they would again
have found areas where they could thrive. In Europe, such
obstacles are the Alps and Carpathians, which blocked the
further northward spread of the Austrian pine *(Pinus nigra)*,
sweet chestnut *(Castanea sativa)*, and Turkey oak *(Quercus
cerris)*. These would otherwise have found favourable conditions
in the warm Rhineland and other regions north of the Alps.
The general pattern of distribution can lead us to deduce that
species found beyond the Arctic Circle, such as birch, pine,
aspen, alder and spruce are frost resistant, whereas species
growing mainly in southern Europe will probably be more
sensitive to cold; in more northern areas only warm and shel-

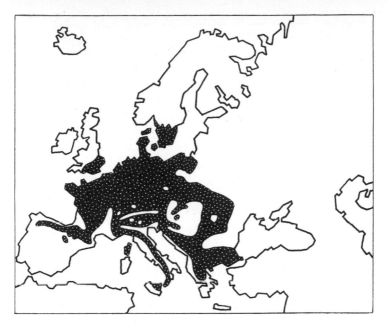

b - beech.

tered sites will be favourable for their growth. When introducing new exotics, a thorough study of their natural environment is the main condition of efficient selection and subsequent, vigorous growth.

Let us take a brief look at the purposes of, and problems associated with, the introduction of exotics. The main reasons for the introduction of new trees from other regions or continents is for their fruit, to increase the yield of timber, or to enrich the assortment of ornamentals. The introduction of new plants dates from long ago; its beginnings can be traced to the cultured peoples of ancient times, who concentrated primarily on the introduction of fruit trees that were important as a source of food. This practice has continued with greater or lesser intensity up to the present day, reaching a peak during the past two centuries when man was settling the vast expanses of the Ameri-

171

cas, Africa and Asia. At first, these plants were imported as novelties for parks and landscape gardens, but, later, economic reasons also prevailed, and exotics were planted in forestry plantations.

Unfortunately, most of these trees and shrubs were set out without any plan, and without sufficient knowledge of their requirements, so that the greater part of these attempts ended in failure. Some successful plantings, however, e.g. the eastern cottonwood, Weymouth pine and Douglas fir, showed how great the economic importance of imported forest trees could be after several decades. The turn of the nineteenth and twentieth centuries thus marked the beginning of a new stage in the planting of imported trees in forests, with due attention being paid to their needs. The results appear to be very promising. For example, the North American giant fir (*Abies grandis* Lindl.) attains an annual increment of 25 to 28 cubic metres of merchantable wood per hectare. In Belgium and France its annual increment is also more than 20 cubic metres per hectare. Similarly, in England, France and Germany the Douglas fir (*Pseudotsuga menziesii* Franco) gives a 40 to 60 per cent higher yield than native species. The largest areas planted with exotic trees and shrubs in woodlands are to be found today in Europe in those countries that have insufficient supplies of their own wood, such as Great Britain and Spain, where there were areas totalling about 250 thousand hectares in 1950. Good results and economic considerations are today forcing the further introduction and planting of exotic trees and shrubs, even in those European countries with large areas of productive forests. A further application has been found for these exotics as ornamental plants in parks and city streets.

The introduction of exotic trees and shrubs, however, has attracted much opposition. The main reason for this opposition is the fear of new diseases, and the fear of changing the characteristic aspect of the landscape. The first can be prevented by systematic checking of imported seeds and plants and of pests on the new plantings. The second can be avoided, if new plants are set out wisely and with forethought. Naturally, imported trees and shrubs should not be planted in the immediate vicinity of nature reserves and in important landscape areas. Most of them differ very little from native species at first glance, and the layman is hard put to distinguish the Sitka spruce and Douglas fir from the Norway spruce or giant fir and the Caucasian fir from the European silver fir. Furthermore, the Ice Age in Europe greatly limited the assortment of species. Most of the genera found in America grew also in Europe at one time, e.g. *Sequoia*, *Tsuga*, *Carya*, *Juglans*, *Liriodendron*, etc., so that their rank as exotics in this area is of only recent date. The augmentation of Europe's assortment of trees and shrubs is, therefore, only the remedying of the results of natural catastrophes, and it is not totally contrary to the natural scheme of things. The main mountain ranges in Europe, the Pyrenees, Alps and Carpathians, run from west to east. During the Ice Age, many trees were blocked by these mountains in their southward retreat before the advancing ice sheet. In America, where the main mountain ranges run from north to south, there was no such barrier, and all the trees that moved south were able to return again to the more northerly regions in the period following the Ice Age. That is why trees that perished in Europe survived in America and also why genera occurring on both continents are much more numerous in the New World.

Exotic trees and shrubs can also be put to good use in parks and city streets. They not only brighten such places and make them more varied, but are, in addition, a source of instruction, enabling nature lovers to expand their knowledge of the plants of other lands. The well-planned introduction of exotics, therefore, is in no way harmful; on the contrary, it can be very rewarding, both from the economic and the cultural aspect.

PRODUCTS WHICH TREES PROVIDE

The principal raw material yielded by trees is wood, which can be used in many ways and for many purposes and which, along with coal — the product of trees of earlier geological periods — made possible the smelting of ores and the development of all branches of industry.

Trees grown for their wood are cultivated in forests. Unlike other raw materials where the supplies are exhausted after a time, if felling is wisely planned, the supply of wood in a forest remains constant and the felled wood is replaced by new wood in the form of new growth. In the mild climate of central and western Europe, the annual increment per hectare, depending on the site, type of soil and prevailing species, averages from three to ten cubic metres of wood that can be cut without decreasing the supply and production of further wood. With systematic care and fertilization this increment can be increased even further, as is shown by the plantations of cultivated hybrid poplars with an annual increment of fifteen to twenty-five cubic metres of merchantable wood.

Felled wood is processed in two ways: mechanically, whereby only the shape is changed, and chemically, whereby not only the shape is changed but also the substance. Wood processed by the first method is used mainly in the building industry, the joinery trade, furniture making, wheel and waggon making, in mines, on railway lines, etc. The favoured wood of the building industry is that of conifers: spruce, pine, fir and larch. It is long, light, well suited for beams, columns, sawn wood, doors, window-boxes and in building ships and transport vehicles. In the furniture industry, it is mainly the wood of broad-leaved trees such as oak, elm, walnut, ash, beech, cherry and certain tropical exotics that is used to make the finer, more delicate pieces. In recent decades, only thin layers, called veneers, of these costly woods are being used; they are glued onto the main structure made of soft wood, thus making the final product not only lighter but also less expensive.

In chemical processing, the wood is either burned by the process of dry distillation, with no air present, or else is decomposed by various chemical agents. Originally, it was burned by the primitive method of the charcoal-stack, which yielded only charcoal used in the melting of ores and iron working. All other valuable products escaped either into the ground or the atmosphere. Today, it is distilled by modern methods, and it is the by-products, such as wood alcohol, vinegar, acetone and pitch oils — and not charcoal — that are of prime importance. It is mainly the hardwoods such as beech, oak, birch, maple and hornbeam which are used for industrial processing.

The chief product of the chemical decomposition of wood is cellulose, used in the manufacture of paper, textiles, guncotton and other products. The wood of spruce, fir, various pines, and poplar and, to a lesser degree, that of beech and birch is used mostly for this purpose. The proportion of wood processed by chemical means is growing rapidly. The papermills of the developed countries, for example, consume large areas of forest every month.

Other raw materials yielded by trees are essential oils, rosin and turpentine. These are obtained from live trees by boring holes in the outer layer of wood or bark, and catching the oils in containers placed beneath them. The best species of trees for this purpose are various pines, larches, and, in sub-tropical regions, members of the genera *Agathis*, *Shorea* and *Canarium*. Similar methods are used in the case of certain tropical, broad-leaved trees to obtain caoutchouc and latex, which are of importance in the rubber, textile and food industries — trees of the genera *Hevea*, *Castilloa*, *Mimusops*, *Achras*, etc.

The leather industry could not function without tannins, another product of many woody plants. In some trees, these are obtained from the bark (spruce, oak), in others from the wood and bark (chestnut, false acacia), and in still others from the leaves (staghorn sumach) or fruits (sapan). Before the day of synthetic dyes, trees were also an important source of natural dyes.

The pharmaceutical industry is another that looks to trees for a number of important substances, though as yet it is only beginning to make a thorough study of the possibilities they offer. Nevertheless, the lives of tens of millions of people have been saved by quinine, for example, extracted from the bark of the cinchona, a tree growing in the sub-tropics.

Trees are also a source of various other raw materials, e.g. cork from the cork oak and the Amur cork tree, and cotton and stuffing material (kapok) from various species of *Ceiba*, the kapok and silk cotton trees.

The fruits and leaves of trees are used to prepare various beverages such as coffee, cocoa, tea, and Coca-Cola, and there are many trees that provide us with edible fruits, either fleshy fruits, such as lemons, oranges, figs, dates, apples, pears, plums and cherries, or oily ones, such as walnuts, hazelnuts, almonds and chestnuts. Today, all these fruits are a good and welcome supplement to our daily fare, but in former times they played a vital role in man's diet. In some undeveloped tropical regions they are the chief source of food to this day.

OTHER USEFUL FUNCTIONS OF TREES

Today, we realize that, besides being a source of raw materials, trees are of even greater importance for their role in the regulation of climate, water management, hygiene, health, recreation; and, last but not least, in beautifying the environment. The past century has witnessed a rapid increase in world population, and the progress of science and technology has greatly changed man's way of life. The result has been the emergence of vast industrial and suburban areas, with the majority of people living in cities, which have a specific climate and air polluted with dust, gases and other noxious substances. Industrial centres and cities are plagued by increasing noise that goes beyond bearable limits, the work pace is accelerating and man's nervous system is being exposed to ever greater stresses and strains. The outlook for the future is one of further increase of population, further mechanization of life, higher consumption of water, increasing noise and greater loads on man's nervous system. With such prospects in view, the role of trees, shrubs and other plants in cities will be of increasing importance, forests will have an increasingly significant role in water management, and people will seek respite from the stress of their daily lives in the country amidst the green of grass, shrubs and trees.

Investigations have shown that plants, and above all trees, reduce the dryness of the city climate. In streets, squares and parks they not only provide shade but also lower the ambient temperature as heat is taken up by the process of photosynthesis and transpiration. At night, conversely, they reduce the radiation of warmth into the atmosphere. Tree belts and expanses of turf enable better penetration of water into the soil, the water then being returned again by them to the atmosphere in the form of vapour during the process of transpiration and evaporation. That is why the ambient temperature is always lower and the relative humidity higher in parks and tree-lined streets.

Trees with a large leaf surface are similarly efficient filters of polluted city air. Their leaves, especially if they are tomentose and covered with fine hairs, entrap large quantities of dust particles, which are then washed off onto the ground by rain. The fact that trees and shrubs lower the speed of wind in city streets also promotes the settling of dust and the clearing of the air. Rows of trees and shrubs between traffic lanes or between street and sidewalk lower the noise of traffic by as much as 10 to 15 per cent.

The effect of tree belts or forest areas promoting the absorption of rainwater is very well known. In a forest, even after a heavy downpour, the water soaks rapidly into the ground and does not form puddles. The chief reason behind this is the soil structure: forest litter, high humus content and the small channels left in the soil by decayed roots. Tree belts also help to prevent erosion and the washing away of soil particles into brooks and rivers, thus not only holding in place the fertile topsoil so vital to good farming, but also keeping various man-made waterworks and reservoirs from being inundated with eroded material. Trees are also an effective means of strengthening the banks of water courses and keeping them from crumbling and washing away. A covering of trees and shrubs also prevents the formation and widening of gullies and ravines in danger spots on the earth's surface.

High up in the mountains, trees and dwarf pine hold back build-ups of snow, thus preventing the formation of the avalanches, that are a common occurrence on treeless slopes when there is a thaw, leaving devastation in their wake and often taking their toll in human lives as well.

Trees in the landscape are pleasing to the eye and an important ornamental element, as one realizes only too well when travelling mile after mile through flat countryside with only the horizon in sight. Trees brighten the landscape and give it its individual character. The broad valleys of large rivers are hard to envisage without groves of poplars amidst the spreading meadows, or without tree-shaded pools. In hill country we are accustomed to see oaks, limes and maples beside farmhouses and churches, and in mountain pastures the occasional mountain ash, juniper and spruce. Beside mountain cottages one may see spreading sycamores, ashes, elms and beeches. Avenues alongside roads and highways not only help these to blend well with the landscape but also provide welcome shade to both man and beast.

The isolated veterans scattered throughout the countryside, chiefly on hills or at crossroads, are an indication of the role they played in the lives of our ancestors and the instinct these men had for their appropriate location. Age-old trees, whose spreading branches offered welcome shade to farmers taking a rest from their toil in the fields one or two hundred years ago, today offer the same welcome respite to urban man seeking relaxation in the countryside. When we stand in awe before these giant and majestic trees, we realize that they are as much a part of a nation's cultural heritage as are outstanding buildings, paintings and sculptures, and other artistic works; and that it is, therefore, our duty and responsibility to preserve them for posterity.

BIBLIOGRAPHY

Acworth, W. Barbara: *Trees for Towns*. London, 1960

Bailey, L. H.: *The Cultivated Conifers*. London, 1933

Bean, W. J.: *Ornamental Trees for Amateurs* (revised and enlarged). London, 1959

Bean, W. J.: *Trees and Shrubs Hardy in the British Isles* (8th edition, revised). London, 1970

Brimble, L. J. F.: *Trees in Britain*. London, 1946

Brockman, C. F. and Zim, H. S.: *Trees of North America*. New York, 1968

Caborne, J. M.: *Shelter Belts and Windbreaks*. London, 1966

Dallimore, W. and Jackson, B.: *A Handbook of Coniferae*. 4th ed. London, 1966

Edlin, H. L.: *Tree Planting and Cultivation*. London, 1970

Edlin, H. L.: *Trees, Woods and Man*. London, 1965

Elwes, H. J. and Henry, A. H.: *The Trees of Great Britain and Ireland*. I. and II. London, 1969

Hadfield, Miles: *British Trees, A Guide for Everyman*. London, 1957

Harlow, W. H. and Harrar, E. S.: *Textbook of Dendrology*. New York, 1958

Jay, B. A.: *Conifers in Britain*. London, 1952

Lloyd, Christopher: *Shrubs and Trees for Small Gardens*. London, 1966

Makins, F. K.: *The Identification of Trees and Shrubs*. London, 1948

Menninger, Edwin A.: *Fantastic Trees*. New York, 1967

Osborn, A.: *Shrubs and Trees for the Garden*. London, 1945

Pokorný, J.: *Trees of Parks and Gardens*. 2nd ed. London, 1970

Prime, C. T. and Deacock, R. J.: *Trees and Shrubs, Their Identification in Summer and Winter*. London, 1951

Rehder, Alfred: *Manual of Cultivated Trees and Shrubs* (hardy in North America) (2nd revised edition). New York, 1958

INDEX OF COMMON NAMES

INDEX OF LATIN NAMES